The Creative Spiralizer Cookbook

The Creative Spiralizer Cookbook

100 Delicious and Filling Spiralized Recipes

By Lauren Mcdonnell

Table of Contents

Spiralizer 101

What is a Spiralizer?

It's a kitchen tool that easily makes noodles out of vegetables. Some models make vegetable ribbons and curls too, in addition to the noodles. One really great thing about these tools is that they're very affordable, with the average price right around twenty dollars.

What types of spiralizers are there?

Handheld spiralizers
This is the cheapest option, much like a large pencil sharpener. Hard work to use for all but very small quantities and will take only vegetables with a diameter of around 2"/5cm or less.

Horizontal hold spiralizers
These manage much larger diameter vegetables than the handheld devices — great for celeriac. However, most hold the vegetables in place with a small metal ring, which cuts a core the size of a pencil from the centre as you turn the mechanism – a bit wasteful, especially for narrower vegetables. More importantly, even with the help of the metal ring, the vegetable tends to slip out of place, which can be infuriatingly as you cut.

Vertical hold spiralizers
These are the best option. The vegetable sits on top of the blade so it's easier to use – there's no risk of the vegetable falling out of position, plus naturally exerting pressure downwards as you turn the handle means it works faster. A spike holds the vegetable in place, so there's no core cut out, and no wastage. It generally take a slightly smaller diameter and shorter length of vegetable than the horizontal.

What Is Spiralizing?

Spiralizing is the art of turning vegetables and fruits into noodles. It really is as simple as that, but so revolutionary. Spiralized vegetable pasta or "Inspiralized" pasta is inherently gluten-free, paleo, vegan and vegetarian friendly, low carb friendly, and of course, it's a cleaner, more wholesome way to eat. Spiralized pasta is not only nutritious and filling, it's easy to make. Spiralizing is for all ages, diet lifestyles and skill levels. The spiralizer allows you to transform a healthy, low-calorie, low-carb vegetable into a giant bowl of pasta! Top with the right sauce and protein and you've got a delicious meal that won't break the diet bank– in minutes.

What are the best vegetables to spiralize?

There are a few vegetables that were born to be spiralized. The firm texture of root vegetables makes them perfect for spiralizing, but you can also use cucumbers, squash or pumpkin, or firm fruits such as apples and pears.

Courgette
Forget spaghetti, its all about 'courgetti.' Use the thin noodle attachment on the spiralizer to create long twirls of pasta-like vegetable noodles. Simply boil the spiralized courgette for 20 seconds, then top with Bolognese or stir through pesto and some prawns.

Carrots
Raw carrot ribbons, made with the slicing blade, add texture and crunch to a salad or slaw. Or, you can stir-fry the carrot ribbons for a couple of minutes with garlic and coconut oil for a healthy side dish.

Sweet potato
Use the thicker noodle blade to create sweet potato curly fries, toss in a little oil and bake until crisp.

Apple
Coleslaw will never be the same again. You can add texture and sweetness with apple noodles; just make sure that you toss them in lemon juice as soon as the apple noodles come out of the spiralizer to prevent them from browning.

Mooli
This large, white vegetable is part of the radish family and is used widely in Asian cooking. Use in place of rice noodles to make pad Thai or use raw in Asian salads.

Which Spiralizer Should I Get?

Hand-held peelers require a little elbow grease, but win on the price and storage front. Heavy-duty stand spiralizers are easier and quicker to use, and while imported versions from the gadget's birthplace – Japan – can cost a pretty penny, there are now several spiralizers on the US market that tend to carry more budget-friendly price tags.

Factors to consider when purchasing a spiralizer

Ease of use: In the case of stand and hand-held spiralizers, you should be able to attach your fruit and vegetables easily, then use a simple lever or twist motion to speedily create ribbons without having to exert too much force.

Resilience: As you want to shred and spiralize harder vegetables, it is important the gadgets are strong and durable – a wobbly handle or flimsy blade won't pass muster when it comes to creating sweet potato or celeriac matchsticks.

Ease of cleaning: You should look for stand spiralizers with removable components that can be washed in a dishwasher or with an old-fashioned manual scrub.

Ease of storage: While flat mandolines and pint-sized peelers will always have the edge when it comes to the size factor, consider compact stand and hand-held spiralizers than can be tucked away neatly.

Features: Any added bonuses, like different shaped blades to allow for various ribbon thicknesses, can be taken into account – ideally a spiralizer can create thin spirals, slices and spaghetti shapes and has attachments that are easy to affix, remove and store.

Spiralizing Alternatives

Julienne Peeler
You can go to your local houseware store (or sometimes they sell them in grocery stores!) and buy a julienne. It can be used to make veggie pasta salad/slaw and zucchini pasta. Simply "peel" the zucchini with the peeler and voila – little veggie "pasta" strips!

Knife
This is a bit more time consuming, but it can be done. Basically, you need to keep slicing your zucchini into smaller and smaller strips to achieve the pasta "shape".

Peeler
There are many types of vegetable peelers (even potato peelers!) and the more heavy duty you get, the better, because the "peels" that it will slice will be thicker. A peeler makes pappardelle type "noodles".

How to Use a Spiralizer

Using a spiralizer is quite simple. These kitchen accessories come in a number of forms, from standalone units to KitchenAid attachments. In general, the spiralizer will have a spot through which to feed your produce items. Choose symmetrical, long, circular-shaped veggies like zucchini, broccoli stems, and potatoes (just cut off the top ends to create a cylindrical shape). As you feed the item through, the spiralizer will turn it into whatever noodle or rice shape you please.

Procedure

If you're using a spiralizer with multiple blades, start by inserting the 1/8-inch spacing blade (this should be the blade with the smallest holes).

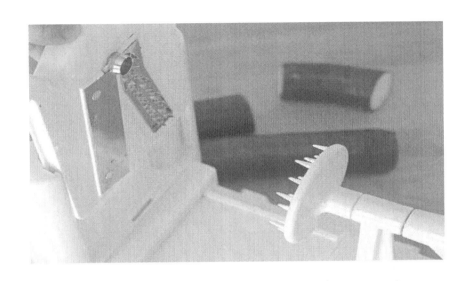

Trim the ends off the fruit/vegetable you wish to spiralize.

Center the fruit/vegetable on the sprializer.

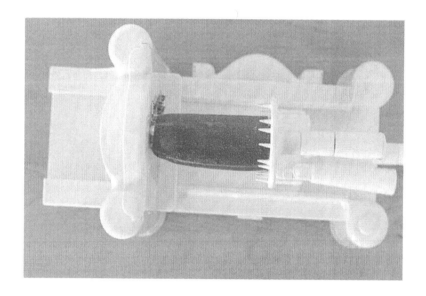

Turn the handle.

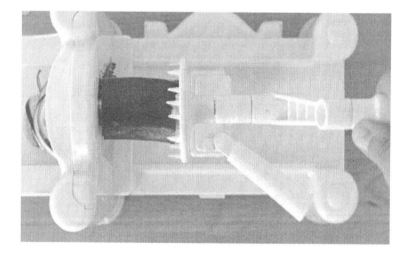

Enjoy your spiralized product.

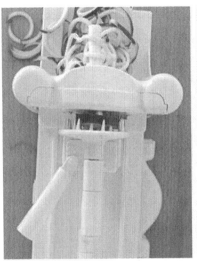

Cleaning and Care

Step #1:
Use a hard brush to wash the handle.

Step #2:
Remove the blades from the Spiralizer and use the same brush to clean the blades. Use caution, as the blades are sharp.

Do not wait hours after using the Spiralizer, if you wash the blade directly after you used it or after you eat an healthy meal, it will be easy to clean with a brush. Be extra careful if you are using anything other than a brush.

Step #3:
Use a brush to wash the body of the spiralizer (you may also use a sponge on this part of the body, as there aren't any blades.)

Step #4:
Place everything on a towel to dry. Once it is dry, assemble and store in your kitchen. It is now ready to be used again.

Salads and Raw Dishes

Greek salad with Cucumber Noodles

Total time: 10 -15 minutes
Servings: 2 – 3

Ingredients
- 2 seedless english cucumbers
- 1 cup grape tomatoes, halved
- 1/3 cup pitted kalamata olives, chopped
- 1/4 of a small red onion, thinly sliced
- 4 tablespoons Sabra Classic Hummus
- 1/2 cup crumbled feta cheese
- salt and black pepper, to taste

Directions
- Use the Inspiralizer to make the cucumber noodles.
- Divide the cucumber noodles onto plates.
- Top with tomatoes, olives, and red onion.
- In the center of the noodles add a spoonful of hummus.
- Sprinkle feta cheese over the noodles.
- Season with salt and black pepper, to taste.
- Serve immediately.

Nutritional Information: 1 serving
- 175 calories
- 6g carbs
- 15mg cholesterol
- 16g fat
- 3g protein
- 627mg sodium

Celeriac Pasta with Walnut and Apple Sauce

Total time: 30 minutes
Servings: 2 - 3

Ingredients
For the sauce:
- 1 large apple, cored and cut into chunks
- 3 tablespoons of walnut oil (good olive oil may be substituted)
- 2 tablespoons lemon juice
- 1 tsp sweetener of choice (honey is best)
- 1/2 tsp raw mustard (recipe link below)
- black pepper

For the pasta:
- 1/2 celeriac
- 3-4 tablespoons lemon juice
- 1 small green onion, finely sliced
- Toppings such as pepitas, sunflower seeds, sesame seeds and fresh thyme

Directions
- First peel your celeriac and make your pasta using a spiralizer.
- Toss pasta in 3-4 tablespoonsof lemon juice and set aside.
- To make the sauce, add the ingredients to a blender and process until you get a smooth mix.
- Toss the pasta in the sauce, add toppings of choice and serve fresh.
- Keeps in the refrigerater for 1 - 2 days.

Nutritional Information: 1 serving
- 300 calories
- 38g carbs
- 115mg cholesterol
- 15g fat
- 3g protein
- 250mg sodium

Walnut Dressing, Beetroot Salad, Carrot & Goat's Cheese

Total time: 25 minutes
Servings: 1 - 2

Ingredients
For the salad:
- 2 medium raw beets (pink and red are best)
- 1 medium carrot
- 4-5 slices of goat's cheese or shaved Pecorino cheese

For the dressing:
- ¼ cup walnuts
- ¼ cup extra-virgin olive oil
- 2 tablespoons lemon juice
- 1 small garlic clove, finely diced or grated
- ½ tsp maple syrup or raw honey
- ¼ tsp sea salt
- pinch of pepper

Directions
- Peel and slice beetroots and carrots very thinly or use a spiralizer to make noodlestrips.
- Place dressing ingredients in a food processor, blender or a mortar and pestle and grind until fairly smooth. It's ok to have a few crunchy bits in there.
- Toss beetroot and carrot noodles with 2-3 tablespoons of the dressing (more if you like).
- Top with goat's cheese.

Nutritional Information: 1 serving
- 166 calories
- 18g carbs
- 21mg cholesterol
- 7g fat
- 3.5g protein
- 150mg sodium

Raw Carrot Pasta with Ginger Lime and Peanut Sauce

Total time: 15 minutes
Servings: 4 - 6

Ingredients
For the Carrot Pasta:
- 5 large carrots, peeled and spiraled into noodles
- 1/3 cup roasted cashews or peanuts
- 2 tablespoons fresh cilantro, finely chopped

Ginger-Lime Peanut Sauce:
- 2 tablespoons creamy peanut butter
- 4 tablespoons coconut milk
- 2 tablespoons liquid aminos
- pinch cayenne pepper
- 2 large cloves garlic, finely chopped
- 1 tablespoon fresh ginger, peeled and grated
- 1 tablespoon lime juice
- kosher salt to taste

Directions
To Prepare the Ginger-Lime Peanut Sauce:
- Combine all ingredients in a small bowl and mix together until smooth and creamy.

To Prepare the Carrot Pasta:
- Wash carrots well, peel them, and pat them dry.
- Using your spiralizer, make noodles out of all of the carrots. It will be more difficult to make the noodles once there is only a few inches of carrot left, so you can grate what's left of the carrot.
- Place all carrot noodles into a large serving bowl.
- Pour the Ginger-Lime Peanut Sauce over the noodles and gently toss together (use your hands for this part).
- Serve with roasted cashews (or peanuts) and freshly chopped cilantro.

Kohlrabi, Prawn and Sesame Salad with Dulse

Total time: 20 minutes
Servings: 4

Ingredients
- 1 tablespoon sesame seeds
- 4-5 spiralized ribbons of dulse or other seaweed
- ½ tsp coconut oil
- 1 garlic clove, finely diced
- 1 tsp diced ginger
- 10 raw or pre-cooked prawns (shrimp)
- 1 medium kohlrabi, peeled
- 1 tablespoon diced green/spring onion (scallions)
- Few fresh coriander leaves (cilantro)
- 1 tablespoon Tamari (gluten-free soy sauce)
- 1 tsp fish sauce
- 1 tablespoon lime juice or ½ tsp tamarind paste (lemon could also be used)
- ½ tsp raw honey
- 1 tsp sesame oil
- 1 tablespoon extra-virgin olive oil
- pinch of chili flakes or a little chili sauce (to your taste)

Directions
- Add sesame seeds to a small frying pan and cook on medium heat for a minute or two, until lightly browned. Remove to a bowl to cool.
- Rinse and soak dry seaweed in cold water for 1-2 minutes and cut into smaller strips.
- In the same frying pan, add coconut oil with garlic and ginger. Bring to high heat, stir and add the prawns. Toss and pan fry for about 30 seconds to heat up the prawns or for a minute if you're cooking raw prawns.
- Peel, grate or thinly slice kohlrabi or use a spiralizer. Combine it with prawns, sesame, green onion, dulse and the dressing. Serve with fresh coriander on top.

Nutritional Information: 1 serving

- 377 calories
- 25g fat
- 60 mg cholesterol
- 1560 mg sodium
- 230 mg calcium
- 770 mg potassium
- 12 g sugar
- 16 g protein

Apple Salad with Crispy Prosciutto

Total time: 20 minutes
Servings: 4

Ingredients
- 8 ounces thinly sliced prosciutto
- 2 granny smith apples
- 4 cups baby arugula
- ½ cup chopped roasted almonds

Salad dressing:
- 2 tablespoons olive oil
- 2 tablespoons apple cider vinegar
- 1 tablespoon honey
- 1 teaspoon coarse grain mustard
- 1 teaspoon fresh lemon juice
- ¼ teaspoon salt
- pinch freshly ground black pepper

Directions
- Preheat oven to 400°F
- Arrange prosciutto in single layer on a large baking sheet. Bake 5 - 8 minutes or until crisp. Cool completely.

Salad dressing:
- For dressing, whisk olive oil, vinegar, honey, mustard, lemon juice, and the salt and pepper in a small bowl until well blended. Set aside until ready to use.
- Use a spiralizer to slice your apples into several strips.
- Divide arugula evenly on four salad plates.
- Top with apples, prosciutto and almonds. Drizzle with dressing.

Nutritional Information: 1 serving
- 350 calories
- 38g carbs
- 115mg cholesterol
- 20g fat
- 4g protein
- 150mg sodium

Beet, Orange and Walnut Salad

Total time: 40 minutes
Servings: 4 - 6

Ingredients
- 2 large red beets, ends trimmed
- 2 oranges, peeled and segmented (reserve liquid)
- 1/2 cup crumbled gorgonzola cheese
- ¼ cup toasted, chopped walnuts
- 2 tablespoons thinly sliced fresh basil

Salad dressing:
- 1 tablespoon orange juice, reserved from oranges
- 1 tablespoon red wine vinegar
- 1/2 teaspoon kosher salt
- ¼ teaspoon pepper
- 3 tablespoons olive oil

Directions
- Using a spiralizer, cut the beets into strips. Cut spirals to desired length.
- Place spiralized beets in a bowl of cold water.
- Let soak 30 minutes, changing the water 2 - 3 times to reduce the amount that the beets bleed onto other ingredients.
- Drain the beets and place in a large bowl.

Salad dressing:
- Combine orange juice, vinegar, and the salt and pepper in a small bowl. Whisk in olive oil. Set aside.
- Toss half the dressing with the beets.
- Add orange segments, gorgonzola, walnuts and half the basil.
- Toss gently.
- Add more dressing as needed.
- Sprinkle with the remaining basil.
- Divide salad evenly onto 4 - 6 plates and serve.

Nutritional Information: 1 serving
- 198 calories
- 11g carbs
- 10mg cholesterol
- 16g fat
- 5g protein
- 460mg sodium

Caprese Zucchini Noodle Salad

Total time: 25 minutes
Servings: 4

Ingredients
- 1 large zucchini, ends trimmed and cut into 4 - inch sections
- 1 pint grape tomatoes, halved
- 4 ounces fresh mozzarella, cut into 1/2 - inch cubes
- 2 tablespoons thinly sliced fresh basil
- 2 teaspoons red wine vinegar
- 1/2 teaspoon kosher salt
- ¼ teaspoon pepper
- 2 tablespoons olive oil

Directions
- Cut the zucchini into strips using a spiralizer
- Cook zucchini noodles in salted water boiling for 45 seconds.
- Drain and place in ice water to stop the cooking process.
- When chilled, drain the zucchini noodles.
- Combine the zucchini, tomatoes, mozzarella and the basil in a large bowl.
- Combine vinegar, salt and pepper in a small bowl, then whisk in olive oil.
- Add the dressing to the salad and toss to coat.
- Divide evenly onto four salad plates and serve.

Nutritional Information: 1 serving
- 166 calories
- 5g carbs
- 22mg cholesterol
- 13g fat
- 8g protein
- 477mg sodium

Greek Cucumber Spiral Salad

Total time: 20 minutes
Servings: 4 -6

Ingredients
- 1 large seedless english cucumber, ends trimmed, cut into 4 - inch sections
- 1 pint grape tomatoes halved or 2 cups chopped tomatoes
- 1/3 cup pitted kalamata olives
- 1/4 cup thinly sliced red onion
- 3 ounces feta cheese, crumbled or cut into chunks

Salad dressing:
- 1 tablespoon lemon juice
- 1 tablespoon red wine vinegar
- 3/4 teaspoon kosher salt
- 1/4 teaspoon pepper
- 1/2 teaspoon dried oregano
- 2 teaspoons fresh minced dill or
- 1/2 teaspoon dry
- 1/4 cup olive oil

Directions
- Cut the sliced cucumbers into desired lengths after spiralizing them
- Place the tomatoes, olives, onion and sliced cucumber in a large bowl.

Salad dressing
- Whisk all of the dressing ingredients together, except olive oil, in small bowl.
- Once combined, slowly add the olive oil into the mixture while continuously whisking.
- Toss the dressing with the cucumber salad and top with feta cheese.
- Divide evenly onto 4 -6 salad plates and serve.

Nutritional Information: 1 serving
- 175 calories
- 6g carbs
- 15mg cholesterol
- 16g fat
- 3g protein
- 627mg sodium

Pear Salad with Blue Cheese Dressing

Total time: 15 minutes
Servings: 4

Ingredients
- 2 D'anjou pears, ends trimmed
- 4 cups mixed watercress, frisee and curly endive
- 1/3 cup pumpkin seeds, roasted and salted

Salad dressing:
- 1/2 cup sour cream
- 1 1/2 teaspoons white wine vinegar
- 1 tablespoons buttermilk
- 1 clove roasted garlic, mashed
- 1/4 cup blue cheese, crumbled
- 1/4 teaspoon freshly ground black pepper
- additional blue cheese for topping

Directions
- Slice the pears into strips using a spiralizer.

Salad dressing
- Combine the sour cream, white wine vinegar, buttermilk and garlic in a small mixing bowl.
- Gently fold in blue cheese.
- Season with black pepper.
- Refrigerate until ready to use.
- Can be made a day ahead.

- Divide greens evenly onto four salad plates.
- Arrange 1/2 pear on top and sprinkle with pumpkin seeds.
- Drizzle with blue cheese dressing or pass separately, along with additional blue cheese.

Nutritional Information: 1 serving
- 166 calories
- 21g carbs
- 22mg cholesterol
- 9g fat
- 4g protein
- 168mg sodium

Raw Beet and Apple Salad with Quinoa

Total time: 15 minutes
Servings: 4

Ingredients
- 2 medium size beets (gold or red), scrubbed and ends trimmed
- 2 Fuji or Granny Smith apples
- 4 cups baby arugula
- 1 cup cooked quinoa, cooled
- 4 tablespoons blue cheese, crumbled
- ¼ cup roasted sunflower seeds

Directions
- Combine the olive oil, vinegar, lemon juice, ginger, honey, red pepper and black pepper in jar with tight-fitting lid; shake until well blended. Set aside.
- Using a spiralizer, slice the beet into several strips.
- Slice apples into sections
- Divide arugula evenly among four serving plates.
- Top with beets, apples and quinoa; sprinkle with blue cheese and sunflower seeds.
- Serve with dressing.

Nutritional Information: 1 serving
- 342 calories
- 29g carbs
- 11mg cholesterol
- 23g fat
- 8g protein
- 415mg sodium

Entrée Recipes

Beef and Broccoli Bowl

Total time: 25 minutes
Servings: 4

Ingredients
- 4 tablespoons soy sauce, divided
- 1 tablespoon seasoned rice
- wine vinegar
- 1/2 teaspoons fresh ginger, grated, divided
- 1 teaspoon fresh garlic, minced, divided
- 1/8 teaspoon red pepper flakes (optional)
- 1 pound sirloin steak, thinly sliced
- ¼ cup hoisin sauce
- 3 tablespoons orange juice
- Spiralized broccoli

Directions
- Combine 1 tablespoon soy sauce, rice wine vinegar, 1 teaspoon ginger, 1/2 teaspoon garlic, red pepper flakes in a medium bowl.
- Toss steak with mixture and refrigerate until ready to use.
- Mix together hoisin, orange juice, remaining soy sauce, ginger and garlic in a small bowl; set aside.
- Prepare broccoli by cutting florets into bite-sized pieces (about 5 cups). Trim any stalks off stem and trim bottom 1/2-inch or toughest part of stem off. Peel stem if desired.
- Cut sliced vegetables to desired length.
- Heat 12 - inch nonstick skillet* over medium - high heat and add 1 tablespoon oil.
- Cook half the steak for 3 - 4 minutes or until browned, but not cooked all the way through. Transfer to platter and repeat with rest of steak.
- Add florets, spiralized broccoli and carrot to hot skillet and cook, stirring constantly for 3 minutes.
- Add 1/2 cup water to pan and immediately cover with lid, allow vegetables to steam for 3 - 4 minutes or until most of the water has evaporated and vegetables are almost tender.

- Add beef and sauce to pan and cook, uncovered, until sauce is simmering and beef is cooked through, about 2 - 3 minutes. Stir in green onions.
- Divide rice evenly into four bowls, top with beef and broccoli.
- Garnish with additional green onion, if desired.
- *NOTE: If using an uncoated skillet, increase oil to 2 tablespoons.

Nutritional Information: 1 serving
- 476 calories
- 54g carbs
- 65mg cholesterol
- 12g fat
- 39g protein
- 386mg sodium

Beet Noodles with Ricotta and Parsley Pesto

Total time: 13 minutes
Servings: 2

Ingredients
- 3 beets, spiralized
- 1 tablespoon olive oil
- 2 shallots, thinly sliced
- 1 clove garlic, minced
- 1 tablespoon balsamic vinegar
- 1/2 cup ricotta cheese
- ¼ cup pistachios

Parsley Pesto:
- 1 cup parsley
- 1 clove garlic
- 1 teaspoon lemon zest
- 1 teaspoon lemon juice
- ¼ cup olive oil
- 1/2 teaspoon salt
- 1/2 teaspoon freshly ground pepper

Directions
- Heat 1 tablespoon olive oil in large skillet over medium - high heat.
- Add shallot and garlic and sauté for 1- 2 minutes.
- Add spiralized beets and continue cooking 6 - 8 minutes, until beets begin to caramelize. Stir in balsamic vinegar.

Parsley pesto
- Chop the parsley and garlic into small bits and mix them.
- Add lemon zest, lemon juice, salt and pepper to the mixture and drizzle in some olive oil
- To serve, divide beets evenly between two plates.
- Top each plate with ¼ cup ricotta, 2 tablespoons pistachios and 2 - 3 teaspoons of parsley pesto.
- Add more pesto as desired.

Nutritional Information: 1 serving

573 calories
24g carbs
32mg cholesterol
49g fat
13g protein
808mg sodium

Butternut Squash Mac and Cheese

Total time: 1 hour 15 minutes
Servings: 8 - 10

Ingredients
- Nonstick cooking spray
- 2 butternut squash - neck only, cut into 4 - inch sections, ends trimmed
- ¼ cup butter + 1 tablespoon, divided
- ¼ cup all-purpose flour
- 1/2 teaspoon kosher salt
- 1/2 teaspoon white pepper
- 1/2 teaspoon ground mustard 21/2 cups low fat milk
- 1 cup (4 ounces) shredded Cheddar cheese
- 1 cup (4 ounces) shredded Gruyere cheese
- 3/4 cup panko bread crumbs

Directions
- Spiralize the squash.
- Preheat oven to 375F
- Arrange oven rack to center position.
- Prepare 2 - quart baking dish with nonstick cooking spray or grease with additional butter.
- Cut spiralized squash into desired lengths.
- Arrange the squash in the prepared baking dish. Dish will be very full. Squash will soften and compress while cooking.
- Melt ¼ cup butter in medium saucepan over medium heat.
- Whisk in flour, salt, pepper and mustard.
- Cook, stirring frequently, for 2 minutes, or until bubbly.
- Add milk a little at a time and continue to whisk until mixture thickens, about 3 - 5 minutes.
- Remove pan from heat; stir in Cheddar and Gruyere cheeses until melted and smooth.
- Pour cheese sauce over squash.
- Cover dish with foil and bake for 45 minutes.
- Melt remaining 1 tablespoon butter in small bowl.
- Stir in the bread crumbs and set aside.
- When the squash is ready, remove foil from dish and sprinkle with bread crumb mixture.

- Continue to bake, uncovered, for 15 - 20 minutes, or until squash is tender.
- Allow the dish to rest 5 minutes before serving.

Nutritional Information: 1 serving
- 294 calories
- 28g carbs
- 46mg cholesterol
- 16g fat
- 12g protein
- 386mg sodium

Butternut Squash Noodles with Blue Cheese and Sage

Total time: 25 minutes
Servings: 6

Ingredients
- 1 butternut squash - neck only, cut into 4 - inch sections, ends trimmed
- 3 teaspoons olive oil, divided
- 1/2 cup red onion, chopped 1 clove garlic
- ¼ cup chicken or vegetable stock
- 2 tablespoons fresh sage, chopped
- 2 teaspoon parsley, chopped
- 2 teaspoons vinegar
- 2 tablespoons blue cheese, crumbled 1/2 teaspoon salt
- 1/2 teaspoon freshly ground black pepper

Directions
- Preheat the oven to 400°F
- Spiralize the butternut squash.
- Toss the spiralized squash with 1 teaspoon olive oil and spread out on a baking sheet.
- Bake 8 - 10 minutes.
- Remove from the oven and set aside.
- Heat remaining 2 teaspoons olive oil in large skillet.
- Add red onion and garlic and sauté 1 minute.
- Add spiralized butternut squash to skillet, sauté 1- 2 minutes.
- Deglaze pan with stock, simmer 1- 2 minutes.
- Stir in sage, parsley and vinegar.
- Divide evenly onto six plates.
- Sprinkle with blue cheese, season with salt and pepper and serve immediately.

Nutritional Information: 1 serving

- 122 calories
- 7g carbs
- 7mg cholesterol
- 10g fat
- 3g protein
- 329mg sodium

Creamy Zucchini Succotash with Grilled Shrimp Skewers

Total time: 1 hour
Servings: 4

Ingredients
- 1 large zucchini, cut into 4 - inch sections, ends trimmed
- 1 large yellow squash, cut into
- 4 - inch sections, ends trimmed
- 5 strips bacon, cut in ¼ - inch pieces
- 1/2 cup finely chopped shallot
- 1 cup thinly sliced sweet red pepper
- 1/2 teaspoon minced fresh garlic
- 1/2 teaspoon kosher salt
- ¼ teaspoon pepper
- 1/2 teaspoon fresh thyme leaves
- 1/2 cup dry white wine
- 1 cup frozen corn, thawed
- 1 cup frozen edamame, thawed
- 1/2 cup heavy cream
- 1 tablespoon lemon juice, plus more for squeezing
- ⅓ cup chopped flat leaf parsley
- 2 tablespoons torn basil leaves
- Lemon wedges

Shrimp Skewers:
- 1 tablespoon lemon juice
- 1 teaspoon seasoning salt
- ¼ teaspoon pepper
- 1/2 teaspoon minced fresh garlic
- 2 tablespoons oil (canola or safflower)
- 1 pound raw shrimp, peeled, deveined, tails removed
- 8 (8 - inch) bamboo skewers, soaked in water for 30 minutes

Directions
- For shrimp marinade, combine lemon juice, seasoning salt, pepper, garlic and oil in a shallow dish.
- Thread raw shrimp onto soaked bamboo skewers and place skewers in dish, turning to coat shrimp with marinade.
- Refrigerate no longer than 20 minutes, until ready to grill.

- Spiralize some zucchini and yellow squash together.
- Cut the spiralized vegetables into 4 - 6 – inch lengths and set aside.
- Preheat the grill or grill pan to medium - high heat.
- Rub grill grates or grill pan with oil to prevent sticking.
- Heat a 12 - inch skillet over medium heat.
- Add bacon, cook until crispy, about 4 minutes.
- Remove bacon to paper towel lined plate.
- Pour off all but 1 tablespoon of bacon fat.
- Add shallots, peppers and garlic to skillet, season with salt, pepper and thyme and cook 2 - 3 minutes or until softened.
- Add wine to pan and scrape the pan as it heats up, getting any browned bits off of the bottom of the pan.
- Simmer until the liquid is reduced by half, 1- 2 minutes.
- Grill the shrimp, cooking until opaque all the way through, about 5 minutes.
- Remove cooked shrimp to plate and cover with foil to keep it warm.
- Add corn, edamame, spiralized zucchini and squash to shallot mixture.
- Cook, stirring over medium - heat for 4 minutes.
- Add the cream and lemon juice.
- Cook over medium - high heat 2 minutes, stirring constantly, until slightly thickened.
- Stir in the parsley and bacon.
- Divide evenly between four plates, topped with shrimp skewers, torn basil and lemon wedges.

Nutritional Information: 1 serving
- 580 calories
- 37g carbs
- 222mg cholesterol
- 30g fat
- 41g protein
- 740mg sodium

Crunchy Veggie Wrap with Hummus and Avocado

Total time: 20 mins
Servings: 4

Ingredients
- 1/2 large yellow squash or zucchini, cut into 4 - inch sections, ends
- trimmed 1 large carrot, cut into 4 - inch sections, ends trimmed
- 1 teaspoon fresh lemon juice
- 2 teaspoons olive oil
- ¼ teaspoon kosher salt
- 1/8 teaspoon pepper
- 2 tablespoons chopped fresh cilantro 4 (10 - inch diameter)
- tortilla wraps
- 1 cup prepared hummus
- 1/2 cup crumbled feta cheese
- 1 avocado, sliced

Directions
- Using a spiralizer, cut the squash and carrots into several strips.
- In a medium bowl, combine lemon juice, olive oil, salt, pepper and cilantro.
- Add the spiralized squash and carrot to bowl. Toss to coat.
- To assemble wraps, spread each wrap with hummus leaving a 1- inch border at edge.
- Arrange the feta and avocado across center of wrap, leaving a 1- inch border around edge.
- Arrange spiralized squash and carrot over feta and avocado.
- Fold in both sides of wrap. Fold bottom of wrap over filling in the middle, pressing gently, continue rolling up to close.
- Cut in half and serve, or wrap in plastic wrap and refrigerate up to 4 hours.

Nutritional Information: 1 serving

- 380 calories
- 39g carbs
- 17mg cholesterol
- 21g fat
- 12g protein
- 882mg sodium

Italian Meatballs and Zucchini Noodles

Total time: 1 hour 15 minutes
Servings: 12

Ingredients
- nonstick cooking spray
- 2 medium sweet potatoes, ends trimmed, cut into 4 - inch sections
- 3 tablespoons olive oil, divided
- 3/4 teaspoon salt, divided
- ⅓ cup finely chopped shallot
- 5 ounces baby spinach, roughly chopped
- 5 large eggs
- ⅓ cup low fat milk
- ¼ teaspoon pepper
- 1 teaspoon Italian seasoning
- 3/4 cup crumbled feta cheese
- ¼ cup grated Parmesan cheese

Directions
- Preheat oven to 375°F.
- Using a spiralizer, cut the potato into several strips.
- Toss the spiralized sweet potatoes with 2 tablespoons oil and ¼ teaspoon salt in a medium bowl.
- Fit spiralized sweet potatoes into each muffin cavity, dividing evenly.
- Bake in the center of the oven for 20 minutes, or until potatoes are just tender.
- While potatoes are baking, heat 1 tablespoon oil in 12 - inch skillet over medium heat.
- Add shallots, stir until softened, about 1- 2 minutes.
- Sprinkle with ¼ teaspoon salt. Add spinach, stir until spinach wilts completely and moisture has evaporated, about 5 minutes. Remove from heat.
- Attach bowl and wire whip to stand mixer.
- Add eggs, milk, remaining ¼ teaspoon salt, pepper and Italian seasoning.
- Whip on speed 6 until well combined and starting to froth.
- Carefully remove muffin pan from oven.

- Spray sweet potatoes again with nonstick cooking spray, evenly divide the spinach mixture over roasted sweet potatoes and top evenly with feta cheese.
- Pour egg mixture into each cavity, filling about 2/3 full.
- Sprinkle each with Parmesan cheese.
- Bake for 17- 20 minutes or until set in the centers and beginning to brown.
- Serve immediately, or cool and store in refrigerator or freezer.
- To warm, preheat oven to 275°F and heat frittatas for 20 minutes or until heated through.

Nutritional Information: 1 serving
- 234 calories
- 7g carbs
- 438mg cholesterol
- 16g fat
- 16g protein
- 431mg sodium

Lemon Shrimp Scampi with Spiralized Zucchini

Total time: 30 minutes
Servings: 4

Ingredients
- 2 large zucchini, cut into 4 – inch sections, ends trimmed
- 1 pound shrimp, peeled, deveined, tail removed
- 3 tablespoons extra virgin olive oil 3/4 teaspoon kosher salt
- 1/2 teaspoon pepper
- 1/2 cup finely chopped shallot
- 1 teaspoon minced fresh garlic
- 1/2 cup dry white wine
- 1/2 cup heavy cream
- ¼ cup chopped flat leaf parsley
- 2 tablespoons torn basil leaves, plus more for garnish
- 1 tablespoon lemon zest
- 1 tablespoon + 1 teaspoon fresh lemon juice, divided

Directions
- Using a spiralizer, cut the zucchini into several strips.
- Heat large skillet over medium-high heat.
- Add 2 tablespoons olive oil to pan.
- Add shrimp, shallots, garlic, salt and pepper.
- Sauté for 1 minute.
- Remove partially cooked shrimp to plate, cover with foil to keep warm, set aside.
- Continue to sauté shallots and garlic for 1 minute.
- Add wine to skillet and bring to simmer, cook until reduced by half, 1- 2 minutes.
- Add lemon zest, 1 tablespoon lemon juice and cream to skillet, bring to simmer, cook until slightly thickened, 1- 2 minutes.
- In a separate large skillet, heat 1 tablespoon olive oil over medium heat.
- Add zucchini noodles.
- Sprinkle with salt and pepper.
- Sauté zucchini noodles, 2 - 3 minutes or until slightly softened.
- Add the shrimp back to cream sauce, sauté 2 - 3 minutes or until cooked through.

- Stir in parsley, and remaining 1 teaspoon lemon juice into mixture.
- Divide the zucchini noodles evenly among four bowls, topped with shrimp and cream sauce.
- Sprinkle bowls with torn basil.
- Garnish with lemon wedges and basil leaves, if desired.
- Serve immediately.

Nutritional Information: 1 serving
- 321 calories
- 9g carbs
- 191mg cholesterol
- 18g fat
- 25g protein
- 626mg sodium

One Pot Zucchini Primavera

Total time: 1 hour
Servings: 4

Ingredients

- 2 large zucchini, cut into 4 – inch sections, ends trimmed
- 1 yellow onion, peeled and trimmed 2 teaspoons olive oil
- 2 cloves garlic, minced
- ¼ teaspoon red pepper flakes
- 1 cup asparagus, cut into 1- inch pieces
- 1 cup sliced mushrooms
- 1 cup fresh or frozen peas
- 1 cup packed baby spinach
- ¼ cup vegetable broth
- ¼ cup heavy cream
- 1 teaspoon coarse salt
- freshly ground black pepper
- ¼ cup shredded parmesan cheese
- ¼ cup fresh parsley, coarsely chopped

Directions

- Using a spiralizer, slice the zucchini into several strips.
- Spiralize the onions.
- Heat the olive oil in a large skillet over medium - high heat.
- Add the garlic and red pepper flakes; cook 1 minute, stirring constantly.
- Add the onion, asparagus, mushrooms and peas and sauté 2 - 3 minutes or until the onion is softened.
- Add the zucchini and spinach and slowly stir in the broth and cream.
- Bring to a simmer and cook 3 minutes or until vegetables are tender.
- Stir in salt and black pepper, if desired.
- Divide evenly among four serving plates; sprinkle with cheese and parsley.

Nutritional Information: 1 serving

- 200 calories
- 22g carbs
- 25mg cholesterol
- 10g fat
- 9g protein
- 800mg sodium

Peanut Zucchini Noodles

Total time: 20 minutes
Servings: 4

Ingredients
- ¼ cup peanut butter
- 2 tablespoons unseasoned rice vinegar
- 2 teaspoons soy sauce
- 2 teaspoons sugar
- ¼ teaspoon red pepper flakes
- 3 tablespoons hot water
- 2 large zucchini, cut into 4 - inch sections, ends trimmed
- 2 teaspoons olive oil
- 1 clove garlic, minced
- 3 carrots, julienned
- 1 red bell pepper, julienned
- 2 tablespoons chopped peanuts
- 2 tablespoons cilantro, chopped

Directions
- For sauce, combine peanut butter, vinegar, soy sauce, sugar and red pepper in small bowl. Add hot water; whisk until smooth.
- Can be made up to 2 days ahead and stored in the refrigerator.
- Using a spiralizer, slice the zucchini into several strips.
- Heat olive oil in a medium skillet over medium-high heat.
- Add garlic and sauté 30 seconds or until fragrant.
- Add spiralized zucchini, carrots and bell pepper, sauté 3 minutes or until crisp-tender.
- Transfer to a serving bowl and add ¼ cup sauce.
- Toss until well blended. Sprinkle with peanuts and cilantro.
- Serve immediately with additional sauce, if desired.
- *NOTE: For a heartier dish, add grilled chicken strips or shrimp.

Nutritional Information: 1 serving
- 210 calories
- 18g carbs
- 0mg cholesterol
- 14g fat
- 7g protein
- 370mg sodium

Plantain Rice with Chicken and Salsa Verde

Total time: 1 hour
Servings: 4

Ingredients
- 2 firm plantains, peeled and cut into 4 - inch sections
- 1 1/2 teaspoons salt, divided
- 1 teaspoon coarsely ground black pepper
- 1 teaspoon cajun seasoning
- 2 pounds chicken thighs and drumsticks (about 4 each)
- 5 tablespoons olive oil, divided
- 1 clove garlic, minced
- 3 tablespoons sliced shallots
- 1 teaspoon grated lemon peel
- 2 cups chicken broth
- 1 cup mint leaves
- 1 cup parsley leaves
- 1 small serrano pepper, seeded
- 2 whole cloves garlic
- 2 tablespoons white balsamic vinegar

Directions
- Preheat oven to 400°F.
- Using a spiralizer, slice the plantain into several strips until they are finely chopped and resemble rice.
- Combine 1 teaspoon salt, black pepper and cajun seasoning in small bowl; rub over all sides of chicken.
- Heat 1 tablespoon olive oil in large skillet over medium - high heat.
- Cook chicken in batches for 5 - 7 minutes or until browned on all sides, adding an additional 1 tablespoon oil between batches.
- Transfer chicken to plate.
- Heat remaining 1 tablespoon olive oil in same skillet.
- Add shallots and minced garlic; cook 1 minute, stirring constantly.
- Add plantains, remaining 1/2 teaspoon salt and season with additional black pepper, if desired; cook 4 minutes, stirring occasionally.

- Add broth and lemon peel, stirring to scrape up browned bits.
- Top with chicken.
- Bake 30 - 35 minutes or until chicken is cooked through (165°F) and liquid is absorbed.

- **For salsa verde**, combine the mint, parsley, serrano pepper and 2 whole cloves garlic in a food processor.
- Pulse 10 times or until finely chopped.
- With food processor running, add remaining 2 tablespoons olive oil in thin steady stream.
- Transfer to a small bowl and stir in vinegar.
- Serve with chicken and plantains.

Nutritional Information: 1 serving
- 490 calories
- 53g carbs
- 125mg cholesterol
- 30g fat
- 5g protein
- 310mg sodium

Pork Cutlet with Apples and Onions

Total time: 30 minutes
Servings: 4

Ingredients

- 6 granny smith apples
- 1 Vidalia onion
- 2 teaspoons coarse grain mustard
- 1 teaspoon minced fresh thyme
- 1 teaspoon white balsamic vinegar
- 1 tablespoon butter
- 4 thin-cut boneless pork chops
- 1/2 teaspoon salt
- freshly ground black pepper
- 1 teaspoon olive oil

Directions

- Using a spiralizer, slice the apples into several strips and spiralizer the onion.
- Melt the butter in a large skillet over medium heat.
- Add the apples and onion and sauté 6 - 8 minutes or until tender.
- Remove from skillet and keep warm.
- Combine the mustard, thyme and vinegar in a small bowl.
- Season pork chops with salt and pepper.
- Heat olive oil over medium-high heat in same skillet.
- Add pork chops; cook 1- 2 minutes per side.
- Add mustard mixture, stirring to scrape up browned bits.
- Return apples and onions along with any accumulated juices to skillet; simmer 2 - 3 minutes or until heated through.
- Place 1 pork chop each onto four plates and top with apple and onion mixture.
- Serve immediately.

Nutritional Information: 1 serving

- 360 calories
- 21g carbs
- 130mg cholesterol
- 11g fat
- 43g protein
- 420mg sodium

Quinoa Sweet Potato Waffles

Total time: 20 minutes
Servings: 4

Ingredients
- 2 large sweet potatoes, ends trimmed, cut into 4 - inch sections
- 1/2 cup cooked red quinoa
- 1 large egg
- 2 tablespoons almond meal
- 1 teaspoon grated orange peel
- 1/2 teaspoon salt
- ¼ teaspoon ground cinnamon
- 1/2 cup sour cream
- 1/2 teaspoon curry powder
- maple syrup (optional)

Directions
- Preheat a waffle maker.
- Using a spiralizer, slice the sweet potatoes into several strips.
- Place a steamer basket in a large saucepan and fill with water to just below steamer.
- Add the sweet potatoes and steam over high heat until potatoes are very tender.
- Measure 3 cups and transfer to a medium bowl.
- Add quinoa, egg, almond meal, orange peel, salt and cinnamon; mix well.
- Add heaping 1/2 cup batter to waffle maker; cook 8 -10 minutes or until waffle is crisp and well browned.
- Repeat with remaining batter.
- Combine sour cream and curry powder in small bowl.
- Serve waffles with sour cream mixture or maple syrup, if desired.

Nutritional Information: 1 serving
- 190 calories
- 21g carbs
- 65mg cholesterol
- 9g fat
- 6g protein
- 370mg sodium

Root Vegetable Nests

Total time: 30 minutes
Servings: 5

Ingredients
- 1 medium sweet potato, cut into 4 - inch sections, ends trimmed
- 1 medium yukon gold potato, ends trimmed
- 1 large beet, scrubbed and ends trimmed
- 2 teaspoons olive oil, divided
- 1 cup sharp cheddar cheese, shredded
- 1 teaspoon sea salt
- 1/2 teaspoon freshly ground black pepper
- 6 large eggs, poached
- 1 teaspoon chives

Directions
- Preheat oven to 400°F.
- Using a spiralizer, slice the sweet potato, potato and beet into several strips.
- Prepare a baking sheet with 1 teaspoon olive oil. Set aside.
- Toss root vegetables with shredded cheddar cheese, salt and remaining 1 teaspoon olive oil.
- Divide root vegetables evenly into six portions and space evenly on prepared baking sheet.
- Bake until root vegetables are tender and golden brown on bottom, 20 - 25 minutes.
- Place 1 vegetable nest on each plate and top with 1 poached egg.
- Garnish with chives and serve immediately.

Nutritional Information: 1 serving
- 215 calories
- 14g carbs
- 231mg cholesterol
- 13g fat
- 12g protein
- 682mg sodium

Seared Tuna with Kohlrabi Carrot Slaw

Total time: 1 hour minutes
Servings: 4

Ingredients
- 2 medium kohlrabi, peeled
- 2 medium carrots, julienned
- 1 cup shredded celery cabbage or savoy cabbage
- 2 green onions, sliced
- ¼ cup soy sauce
- 1 clove garlic, minced
- 1 teaspoon hot chinese mustard
- 2 tuna steaks (6 ounces each)
- 1 tablespoon vegetable oil
- 1 teaspoon sesame seeds

Dressing:
- 3 tablespoons unseasoned rice vinegar
- 2 tablespoons wasabi powder
- 2 tablespoons fresh lime juice
- 1 tablespoon dark sesame oil
- 11/2 teaspoons agave nectar
- 1/2 teaspoon grated lime peel
- 1/2 teaspoon salt

Directions
- Using a spiralizer, slice the kohlrabi into several strips.
- Add the carrots, the cabbage and the green onions to a bowl.
- Refrigerate until ready to use; can be made up to 6 hours ahead.
- Combine the soy sauce, garlic and mustard in a shallow glass dish.
- Add the tuna and turn to coat.
- Marinate at room temperature for 10 minutes.
- Heat vegetable oil in medium skillet over medium - high heat.
- Add tuna; cook about 2 minutes per side or until desired degree of doneness.
- Transfer to a cutting board and let stand 5 minutes.
- Cut into ¼ - inch slices.

Dressing:
- Combine the vinegar, wasabi powder, lime juice, sesame oil, agave, lime peel and salt in small jar with tight - fitting lid; shake until well blended.
- Refrigerate until ready to use; can be made up to 2 days ahead.

- Divide kohlrabi mixture evenly onto four serving plates.
- Top with sliced tuna, drizzle with dressing and garnish with sesame seeds.

Nutritional Information: 1 serving
- 280 calories
- 18g carbs
- 35mg cholesterol
- 13g fat
- 23g protein
- 1740mg sodium

Sirloin Tacos with Beet Salsa

Total time: 25 minutes
Servings: 4

Ingredients
- 1 sirloin steak (1 pound)
- 12 taco-size flour tortillas, warmed
- 1 1/2 cups shredded romaine lettuce
- 1/2 cup crumbled goat cheese
- 1/2 cup sunflower seeds

Beet salsa:
- 3 golden beets, scrubbed and ends trimmed
- 1 small sweet onion
- 1 tablespoon olive oil
- 1 clove garlic, minced
- 1 jalapeño pepper, seeded and finely chopped
- ¼ cup chopped fresh cilantro
- 1 teaspoon white wine vinegar
- 1/2 teaspoon ground cumin
- 1 teaspoon salt, divided
- 3/4 teaspoon freshly ground black pepper, divided

Directions
- Using a spiralizer, slice the beet and onion into several strips.
- Coarsely chop the beet and onion.

Beet Salsa
- Heat olive oil in a large skillet over medium - high heat.
- Add beets, onions and garlic and sauté about 5 minutes or until beets are tender.
- Transfer to a medium bowl; cool slightly.
- Stir in jalapeño, cilantro, vinegar, cumin, 1/2 teaspoon salt and ¼ teaspoon black pepper.
- Set aside.

- Prepare grill for direct cooking.
- Sprinkle remaining 1/2 teaspoon salt and 1/2 teaspoon black over both sides of steak. Grill, covered, over medium - high heat, 6 - 7 minutes per side for medium-rare, or to desired doneness.
- Transfer to a cutting board and let stand for 10 minutes.

- Thinly slice steak against the grain.
- Divide steak evenly into the tortillas, topped with salsa, lettuce, goat cheese and sunflower seeds.

Nutritional Information: 1 serving
- 590 calories
- 60g carbs
- 70mg cholesterol
- 22g fat
- 36g protein
- 1220mg sodium

Spiralized Pepperoni Pizza

Total time: 1 hour
Servings: 4

Ingredients
- 1 prepared pizza crust (11-12 inches)
- 1 small red onion, peeled and ends trimmed 1 piece (4 - inches) stick pepperoni
- 1/2 cup prepared pizza sauce
- 1 cup (4 - ounces) shredded mozzarella cheese
- ¼ cup shredded parmesan cheese

Directions
- PREHEAT OVEN according to package directions for pizza crust.
- Using a spiralizer, slice the onion and pepperoni into several strips.
- Cut the pepperoni spirals into desired lengths.
- Spread the sauce over the crust to within 1- inch of edge.
- Sprinkle with mozzarella cheese, top with pepperoni and onion.
- Sprinkle with parmesan cheese.
- Bake according to package directions for pizza crust or until cheese is melted and bubbly and crust is golden brown.

Nutritional Information: 1 serving
- 400 calories
- 52g carbs
- 30mg cholesterol
- 13g fat
- 19g protein
- 1240mg sodium

Spiralized Veggie Pizza

Total time: 1 hour
Servings: 4

Ingredients
- 1/2 large zucchini, cut into 4 - inch sections, ends trimmed
- 1/2 large yellow squash, cut into
- 4 - inch sections, ends trimmed
- 1 small red onion, peeled and ends trimmed
- 1/2 teaspoon kosher salt
- 1 pound fresh pizza dough
- (recipe follows), or premade dough 1/2 cup pizza sauce
- 1 teaspoon italian seasoning
- 2 cups shredded mozzarella cheese 1/2 cup thinly sliced sweet red pepper
- 4 teaspoons olive oil

Pizza Dough:
- butter (to grease bowl)
- 1 1/2 – 2 3/4 cups bread flour
- 1/2 teaspoon sugar
- 1¼ teaspoon rapid rise yeast
- 1 teaspoon kosher salt
- 3/4 cup warm water (105°F -115°F)
- 1 tablespoon olive oil

Directions
- Using a spiralizer, slice the zucchini into several strips.
- Repeat with the yellow squash.
- Cut zucchini and squash to desired lengths.
- Place zucchini and squash in a strainer over a bowl.
- Sprinkle with salt and toss.
- Allow to rest for 30 minutes.
- Spiralize the onion.

- On a floured surface, roll out the pizza dough into a 14 -15 inch circle.
- Place on pizza stone or pan.
- Spread sauce on dough leaving a 1- inch border, sprinkle with Italian seasoning.

- Add cheese over sauce.
- Transfer spiralized zucchini and squash from strainer to a paper towel lined surface, place another layer of paper towel on top.
- Gently press to absorb excess moisture.
- Top the pizza with zucchini, squash, onions and peppers.
- Brush the edge of the crust with olive oil and drizzle any extra over pizza toppings.
- Bake the pizza for 20 minutes or until cheese is bubbly and crust is browned.

For Pizza Dough:
- Attach bowl and dough hook to stand mixer.
- Measure 1 1/2 cups bread flour, sugar, yeast and salt together in a bowl.
- Stir together water and olive oil in a liquid measuring cup and pour into the dry mixture.
- Mix on speed 2 until blended and a sticky dough forms, about 3 minutes.
- Add remaining flour, 1/2 cup at a time, until dough clings to hook and forms a ball, about 2 minutes.
- Knead on speed 2 for 2 minutes.
- Grease a medium bowl with butter.
- Place dough in bowl, turning to grease all sides.
- Cover with plastic wrap and allow to rise in a warm place for 1 hour or until doubled in size.
- Punch down dough and form a ball, place on lightly oiled plate and cover loosely with plastic wrap.
- Allow dough to rest for about 30 minutes before shaping.

Nutritional Information: 1 serving
- 295 calories
- 36g carbs
- 16mg cholesterol
- 11g fat
- 13g protein
- 618mg sodium

Sweet Potato Baked Ziti with Mushrooms and Spinach

Total time: 1 hour 20 minutes
Servings: 8 - 10

Ingredients
- nonstick cooking spray
- 2 - 3 medium sweet potatoes, cut into 4 inch sections, ends trimmed
- 1 tablespoon olive oil
- 16 ounces chopped crimini mushrooms
- ¼ cup finely minced shallot
- 1 teaspoon minced fresh garlic
- 1 teaspoon kosher salt, divided
- 1/2 teaspoon pepper, divided
- 1 teaspoon Italian seasoning
- 1 tablespoon balsamic vinegar
- 10 ounces frozen spinach, thawed and squeezed dry
- 16 ounces ricotta cheese
- 2 cups shredded mozzarella cheese, divided
- ¼ cup plus 2 tablespoons grated parmesan cheese, divided

Marinara sauce:
- 1 tablespoon olive oil
- ¼ cup finely minced shallot
- 1 teaspoon minced fresh garlic
- 1/2 teaspoon salt
- ¼ teaspoon pepper
- 1 teaspoon italian seasoning
- 28 ounce can crushed tomatoes

Directions
- Preheat oven to 375°F.
- Prepare a 13 x 9 x 2 baking dish with nonstick cooking spray.
- Heat 1 tablespoon oil in a 12 - inch skillet over medium heat.
- Add shallots, garlic, salt, pepper and italian seasoning.
- Cook, stirring frequently, for 2 minutes or until shallots are softened.
- Add crushed tomatoes and bring to a simmer.

- Reduce heat and stir frequently for 10 minutes or until ready to use.
- Heat 1 tablespoon oil in a separate 12 - inch skillet over medium heat.
- Add mushrooms, shallots, garlic, 1/2 teaspoon salt, ¼ teaspoon pepper and italian seasoning.
- Cook, stirring 7- 8 minutes or until the mushrooms have released their juices and are starting to brown.
- Stir in balsamic vinegar and cook, stirring 1 minute.
- Add spinach and stir into mixture.
- Remove from heat and allow to cool. Set aside.
- Add ricotta cheese, 1 1/2 cups mozzarella cheese, ¼ cup Parmesan cheese.
- Stir in the remaining 1/2 teaspoon salt and ¼ teaspoon pepper into bowl.
- Mix well.
- Add the cooled mushroom and spinach mixture and mix slowly.
- Set aside.
- Using a spiralizer, slice the sweet potato into several strips.
- Repeat with remaining sweet potatoes to yield 8 cups.
- Coat bottom of prepared pan with ⅓ cup marinara sauce.
- Arrange half the sweet potatoes over sauce.
- Add half the ricotta mixture over sweet potatoes and top with half of marinara sauce. Layer remaining sweet potatoes, ricotta mixture and marinara sauce.
- Cover and bake for 45 minutes.
- Uncover, top with remaining Parmesan and mozzarella and bake uncovered for 20 - 25 minutes or until the sweet potatoes are tender.
- Allow to rest for 10 minutes before serving.

Nutritional Information: 1 serving
- 281 calories
- 24g carbs
- 32mg cholesterol
- 13g fat
- 18g protein
- 799mg sodium

Sweet Potato Curry

Total time: 40 minutes
Servings: 8

Ingredients
- 3 medium sweet potatoes, cut in half
- 1 piece (3 inches) lemongrass, coarsely chopped
- 1 teaspoon grated fresh ginger
- 3 cloves garlic
- 3 teaspoons vegetable oil, divided
- 2 cups water
- 1-15 ounce can chickpeas, drained 1-14 ounce can crushed tomatoes
- 1-13 ounce can coconut milk
- 1/2 cup chopped onion
- 1/2 cup chopped carrots
- 3 tablespoons red curry paste
- 1 tablespoon tomato paste
- 1 teaspoon salt
- 1 teaspoon ground coriander
- 4 cups cooked jasmine rice
- ¼ cup chopped fresh basil
- ¼ cup chopped fresh cilantro
- 2 limes, cut into wedges

Directions
- Using a spiralizer, slice the sweet potato into several strips.
- Position a medium bowl under the blades to catch sliced sweet potato and peel.
- Turn stand mixer to speed 4 and process until blade reaches end of sweet potato.
- Repeat with remaining sweet potatoes.
- Set aside.
- Add lemongrass, ginger, garlic and 2 teaspoons vegetable oil in a food chopper.
- Process until finely chopped.
- Set aside.
- Heat remaining 1 teaspoon vegetable oil in large saucepan.
- Add lemongrass mixture; sauté 2 - 3 minutes.

- Stir in water, chickpeas, tomatoes, coconut milk, onion, carrots, curry paste, tomato paste, salt and coriander.
- Add spiralized sweet potatoes; bring to a boil.
- Reduce heat to medium; simmer 25 - 30 minutes or until potatoes are tender and sauce is thickened.
- Divide rice evenly into 8 serving bowls; top with curry, basil and cilantro.
- Serve with lime wedges.

Nutritional Information: 1 serving
- 330 calories
- 47g carbs
- 0mg cholesterol
- 14g fat
- 7g protein
- 640mg sodium

Potato Mac and Cheese

Total time: 1 hour 20 minutes
Servings: 4

Ingredients
- 4 large sweet potatoes, cut into 4 - inch sections, ends trimmed
- 4 tablespoons butter, divided
- 4 tablespoons all - purpose flour
- 2 cups milk
- 2 cups sharp cheddar cheese
- 1/2 teaspoon mustard
- ¼ teaspoon cayenne
- 1/2 teaspoon salt
- 1/2 cup panko breadcrumbs

Directions
- Using a spiralizer, slice the sweet potatoes into several strips.
- Arrange the sweet potatoes in single layer on lightly oiled baking sheet.
- Bake 10 -12 minutes, tossing often, until pierced easily with a fork.
- Melt 3 tablespoons butter in medium saucepan over low heat.
- Add flour, stirring constantly, 2 - 3 minutes.
- Gradually add milk, whisking constantly.
- Increase to medium heat, stirring constantly until thickened, 3 - 5 minutes.
- Add 1 ½ cups cheese, mustard and cayenne and stir until the cheese is melted.
- Remove cheese sauce from heat and set aside.
- Heat remaining 1 tablespoon butter in medium skillet.
- Add panko breadcrumbs and toast until golden, 2 - 3 minutes.
- Set aside.
- Coat 8 x 8 - inch baking dish with butter. In large mixing bowl, combine spiralized sweet potatoes and cheese sauce.
- Transfer mixture to prepared baking dish, top with remaining ½ cup cheese and toasted breadcrumbs.
- Bake until bubbly and crispy, about 40 minutes.

Nutritional Information: 1 serving

- 613 calories
- 54g carbs
- 99mg cholesterol
- 34g fat
- 24g protein
- 963mg sodium

Sweet Potato Risotto

Total time: 25 minutes
Servings: 2

Ingredients
- 2 large sweet potatoes, cut into 4 - inch sections, ends trimmed
- 2 teaspoons olive oil
- ¼ cup chopped yellow onion
- 1 clove garlic, minced
- 1/2 cup vegetable broth
- 1/2 teaspoon salt
- ¼ cup crumbled goat cheese
- 2 tablespoons marcona or roasted almonds, chopped
- 1 teaspoon minced fresh rosemary
- freshly ground black pepper (optional)

Directions
- Using a spiralizer, slice the sweet potatoes into several strips.
- Place spiralized sweet potatoes in a food processor and pulse 6 - 8 times or until sweet potato forms rice-sized pieces.
- If you do not have a food processor, finely chop the spiralized sweet potatoes with a knife.
- Heat 2 teaspoons olive oil in large skillet over medium - high heat.
- Add onion and garlic and sauté 1 minute.
- Add sweet potato and salt and stir to coat with oil.
- Stir in broth, 2 tablespoons at a timeand cook 7-10 minutes or until sweet potatoes are tender.
- Divide risotto evenly between two serving plates.
- Top with goat cheese, almonds and rosemary.
- Season with freshly ground black pepper, if desired.

Nutritional Information: 1 serving
- 250 calories
- 29g carbs
- 15mg cholesterol
- 13g fat
- 7g protein
- 970mg sodium

Pasta and Noodle Recipes

Zucchini Fettuccine with Rosemary Butternut Creme Sauce

Total time: 1 hour 10 minutes
Servings: 4 - 6

Ingredients
- 1 medium butternut squash
- 3 tablespoons coconut oil, divided
- 1 medium yellow onion, chopped
- 2 garlic cloves, minced
- 2 teaspoons dried rosemary, crushed (to release flavor)
- 1 cup full-fat canned coconut milk
- ½ cup vegetable or chicken broth
- ½ teaspoon sea salt
- 1 pound shiitake mushrooms, sliced
- 3 pounds zucchini, spiralized into fettuccine
- freshly-ground black pepper to taste

Directions
- Preheat oven to 375 degrees F.
- Slice butternut squash in half lengthwise.
- Grease a baking sheet with 1 tablespoon of coconut oil and then lay butternut squash (cut side down) on sheet pan.
- Roast for 30 - 45 minutes, until squash is tender and flesh can easily be pierced with a fork.
- Once cooked, allow squash to cool, then scoop out the flesh (this should yield about 5 cups of flesh) and discard the skin.
- Add the flesh to a blender.
- Meanwhile, add 1 tablespoon of coconut oil to a pan over medium heat.
- Add the onions and garlic and saute for 3 - 5 minutes, until onion is translucent and garlic is fragrant.
- Next, add the sauteed garlic and onions, rosemary, coconut milk, broth, and salt to a blender with the butternut squash flesh.
- Blend until smooth.

- Add the remaining tablespoon of coconut oil to a large pan.
- Add the mushrooms and saute for about 2 minutes, until they are just starting to brown. Then add the zucchini fettuccine and cook for about 3 minutes, until zucchini is almost tender.
- Add the sauce to the pan and continue to cook until sauce is hot and zucchini is tender.
- Garnish with freshly-ground black pepper and serve hot.

Nutritional Information: 1 serving
- 270 calories
- 15g total fat
- 85mg cholesterol
- 28g protein
- 9g sugars

Chicken and Chickpea Broccoli Pasta

Total time: 35 minutes
Servings: 3

Ingredients
- 1/2 tablespoon extra virgin olive oil
- 1 boneless chicken breast (about .75 lb)
- salt and pepper, to taste
- ¼ teaspoon dried oregano flakes
- 2 broccoli stems, spiralized
- 1/2 cup canned chickpeas, drained and rinsed
- ½ cup cooked green peas
- 1/2 cup thinly sliced leeks
  For the dressing:
- 2 tablespoons basil, chopped
- 1/3 cup feta
- 1/2 shallot, chopped
- 1 tablespoon lemon juice
- salt and pepper to taste
- 1 tablespoons olive oil
- 1 tablespoons red wine vinegar
- 1 small garlic clove, minced

Directions
- Place a large skillet over medium heat and add in the olive oil.
- Meanwhile, season chicken with salt, pepper and oregano on both sides.
- Once oil is shimmering, add in the chicken and cook until no longer pink.
- Set aside.
- Place a medium pot filled halfway with water over high heat and bring to a boil.
- Once boiling, add in the broccoli noodles and peas and cook for 2-3 minutes or until the broccoli noodles are softened and cooked to al dente and the peas are bright green.
- Drain and set aside.
- While broccoli noodles are chilling, place all of the ingredients for the feta dressing into a food processor and pulse until creamy.

- Place the broccoli noodles, chickpeas, peas, leeks and dressing in a large bowl and toss to combine.
- Serve immediately.

Nutritional Information: 1 serving
- 399 calories
- 15 mg cholesterol
- 5g sugars
- 39g proteins
- 14 total fat

Butternut Squash Noodles in Sage Butter

Total time: 20 minutes
Servings: 4

Ingredients
- 4 cups spiralized butternut squash 'noodles', prepared using the 1/8-inch or 3mm noodle blade*
- 2 teaspoons extra virgin olive oil
- 4 tablespoons unsalted butter
- 10 medium fresh sage leaves
- salt and pepper to taste
- optional garnish: freshly grated Parmesan cheese

Directions
- Preheat oven to 400 degrees F.
- Prepare a large baking sheet with parchment paper.
- Place the spiralized squash noodles on the parchment and drizzle with the olive oil.
- Gently toss to coat with the oil.
- Bake for 7 minutes.
- Noodles will be softer but not completely soft, however they will continue to soften outside of the oven.
- While noodles are cooking, melt the butter in a large skillet over medium heat, stirring constantly.
- Within 1-2 minutes the butter will begin to brown; add the sage leaves at this time, stirring to saute them until they are fragrant and darken.
- The entire process only takes 2-3 minutes.
- Remove from heat.
- Toss the squash noodles in the browned butter to fully coat and serve immediately.

Nutritional Information: 1 serving
- 300 calories
- 17g total fat
- 90mg cholesterol
- 34g protein
- 9g sugars

Slutty Low-Carb Pasta all Puttanesca

Total time: 30 minutes
Servings: 2

Ingredients
- 3 zucchini
- anchovies (you wont taste them, they just give a salty richness to the dish)
- 2 cloves of garlic
- handful of capers
- handful of pitted black olives
- Chili flakes
- Can of tomatoes
- olive oil
- parmesan cheese

Directions
- Get a pan nice and hot, then turn down to a medium heat.
- Add a generous glug of olive oil, enough to coat the bottom.
- Crush two cloves of garlic into the oil.
- Add three or four anchovies.
- The anchovies should start to disintegrate in the oil and the garlic gently brown and soften.
- Add a sprinkle of chilli flakes to the sizzling oil.
- Roughly chop up your black olives and capers and add them too.
- Give it all a good stir around and fry for a minute.
- Add your canned tomatoes.
- Let it all bubble away, stirring now and then for a few mins.
- Then put on one side to cool.
- Using a spiralizer or a funny mandolin attachment, cut your zucchini into ribbons.
- Toss the sauce through your Zoodles.
- Serve with some fresh parmesan.

Nutritional Information: 1 serving

- 1036 calories
- 62g total fat
- 158mg cholesterol
- 91g protein

Daikon Noodle Soup with Broccolini and Asian Pork Meatballs

Total time: 35 minutes
Servings: 4

Ingredients
For the meatballs:
- 1 pound lean ground pork
- 1 teaspoon peeled and minced ginger
- 1/3 cup chopped scallions
- 1 tablespoon soy sauce
- 1 teaspoon finely minced garlic
- 3 teaspoons chopped cilantro
- salt and pepper, to taste

For the soup:
- 1 teaspoon sesame oil
- 1 tablespoon peeled and minced ginger
- 2 bunches broccolini, halved (make sure to cut off any rough ends on the stems) pepper, to taste
- 4 cups chicken broth
- 2 cups water
- 1 tablespoon soy sauce
- 1 tablespoon fish sauce
- 2 teaspoons chili sauce or sriracha
- 3 medium daikon radishes, spiralized
- ½ cup cilantro leaves

Directions
- Preheat the oven to 400 degrees and line a baking sheet with parchment paper.
- Place all of the ingredients for the meatballs into a large bowl and mix together.
- Form 10-12 golf ball sized meatballs with hands and place on the parchment paper.
- Bake until cooked through, about 18 minutes.
- Once you place the meatballs in the oven to bake, place a large saucepan over medium heat and add in the sesame oil.
- Once oil heats, add in the ginger, cooking for 30 seconds or until fragrant.

- Add in the broccolini, season with pepper and cook for 3-5 minutes or until it turns bright green.
- Add in the chicken broth, water, soy sauce, fish sauce and chili sauce.
- Cover and bring to a boil and then uncover, lower heat and simmer for 10 minutes until broccolini is crisp-tender.
- Then, add in the daikon noodles and cook for 3-5 minutes or until noodles are to your preference (if you like al dente, no more than 3 minutes, if you like softer, go up to 5 minutes.)
- Portion the soup into bowls, top with 3 golf ball sized meatballs.
- Garnish with cilantro and serve immediately.

Nutritional Information: 1 serving
- 292 calories
- 13g total fat
- 74mg cholesterol
- 28g protein
- 9g sugars
- 1424mg sodium

Zoodles and Meatballs

Total time: 20 minutes
Servings: 3

Ingredients
- 12 meatballs and sauce (1/2 batch)
- 1 tablespoons extra virgin olive oil
- 1/4 cup red onion, diced
- 3 cloves garlic, minced
- 3 (8 oz each) zucchinis, cut into long julienne strips (with a mandolin or spiralizer) salt and fresh cracked pepper, to taste

Directions
- Heat a large nonstick skillet over medium heat.
- When hot add the oil, onions and garlic and cook until fragrant, about 1 to 2 minutes.
- Increase heat to medium-high and add the zucchini, season with salt and pepper to taste and cook about 1 minute.
- Give it a stir to mix everything around and cook another 1 to 1-1/2 minutes, or until the vegetables are cooked through yet firm.
- Divide the zucchini between three bowls and top with four meatballs and sauce, add some grated cheese and enjoy!

Nutritional Information: 1 serving
- 325 calories
- 15g fat
- 25g carbs
- 7g fiber
- 25g protein
- 4g sugar

Garlic-parmesan Zucchini Noodles and Spaghetti Pasta

Total time: 25 minutes
Servings: 2

Ingredients
- 2 ounces of spaghetti
- pinch of salt
- 3 medium garlic cloves
- 3 tablespoons extra virgin olive oil
- ¼ teaspoon red pepper flakes
- 1 medium zucchini
- 3 tablespoons grated parmesan cheese
- salt and pepper, to taste

Directions
- Bring a large pot of water and a pinch of salt to a boil.
- Once boiling, drop in the spaghetti and cook until al dente, per package directions (typically 10 minutes.)
- While the pasta is cooking, thinly slice the garlic and spiralize your zucchini.
- Trim the noodles using scissors.
- Set both aside.
- When the pasta is ready, drain it and set aside, discarding the pasta water.
- Place a large skillet on medium heat and pour in the oil.
- Add the garlic and chili flakes and cook for 30 seconds or until garlic is fragrant.
- Add in the zucchini noodles and toss for 2-3 minutes or until al dente.
- Then, add in the "real" spaghetti and season generously with salt and pepper.
- Remove the skillet from the heat and add in the parmesan cheese.
- Toss until cheese is melted into the pasta.
- Serve immediately.

Nutritional Information: 1 serving

- 344 calories
- 25g total fat
- 8mg cholesterol
- 3g sugars
- 9g proteins

Ginger Zucchini Noodle Egg Drop Soup

Total time: 25 minutes
Servings: 4 - 6
Ingredients
- 4 medium to large zucchini
- 2 tablespoons extra virgin olive oil
- 2 tablespoons minced ginger
- 5 cups shiitake mushrooms, sliced
- 8 cups vegetable broth, divided
- 2 cups, plus 1 tablespoon water, divided
- ½ teaspoons red pepper flakes
- 5 tablespoons low-sodium tamari sauce or soy sauce
- 2 cups thinly sliced scallions, divided
- 4 large eggs, beaten
- 3 tablespoons corn starch
- salt & pepper to taste

Directions
- Prepare the zucchini noodles with a spiralizer.
- In a large pot, heat the olive oil over medium-high heat.
- Add the minced ginger and cook, stirring, for 2 minutes.
- Add the shiitake mushrooms and a tablespoon of water and cook until the mushrooms begin to sweat.
- Add 7 cups of the vegetable broth, the remaining water, the red pepper flakes, tamari sauce, and 1½ cups of the chopped scallions.
- Bring to a boil, stirring occasionally.
- Meanwhile, mix the remaining cup of vegetable broth with the corn starch and whisk until completely smooth.
- While stirring the soup, slowly pour in the beaten eggs in a thin stream.
- Continue stirring until all of the egg is incorporated.
- Slowly pour the corn starch mixture into the soup and cook for about 4-5 minutes to thicken.
- Season to taste with salt & pepper.
- Add the spiralized zucchini noodles to the pot and cook, stirring, for about 2 minutes, or until the noodles are just soft and flexible (remember, they'll continue cooking in your bowl!).
- Serve topped with the remaining scallions.

Baked and Warm Recipes

Baked Sweet Potato Curly Fries

Total time: 25 minutes
Servings: 2

Ingredients
- 1 large sweet potato
- olive oil
- kosher salt (I like Redmonds Sea Salt)

Directions
- Preheat oven to 400 degrees and line a baking sheet with foil.
- Peel sweet potato and cut off each end to make a flat surface to attach to the prongs.
- Secure spiralizer to the counter top and attach potato, as centered as possible, to the spiralizer.
- Twist the handle to make curly fries.
- Clean out potato and remove core from the spiralizer.
- Drizzle curly fries in olive oil and toss to coat.
- Shake salt over fries.
- Bake for 20-25 minutes. (Fries in the corner of the pan will get a bit more crispy--but I like that.)
- Allow to cool for a few minutes, serve immediately.

Sweet Potato Noodle Buns

Total time: 45 minutes
Servings: 1

Ingredients
- 1 sweet potato, peeled and ends cut flat
- 2 tsp olive oil, divided
- 1 large egg
- pinch kosher salt
- pinch freshly ground black pepper

Directions
- Using a spiralizer, cut sweet potato into thin strands.
- In a large skillet, heat 1/2 tsp (2 mL) oil over medium heat.
- Add sweet potato and cook, stirring, for 5 to 7 minutes or until softened.
- Let cool to room temperature, about 15 minutes.
- In a medium bowl, whisk egg. Stir in sweet potato, salt and pepper.
- Divide between prepared ramekins, filling each about halfway and pressing the sweet potato down into the ramekins.
- Cover with plastic wrap and place a heavy can or jar on top of the wrap to weigh down the sweet potato.
- Refrigerate for 30 minutes.
- Lightly coat a skillet with the remaining oil and heat over medium-high heat.
- Remove plastic wrap and invert ramekins to slide noodle buns onto skillet.
- Cook, turning once, for 3 to 5 minutes per side or until golden brown on both sides and hot in the center.

Savoury Latkes (potato pancakes)

Total time: 45 minutes
Servings: 2 - 3

Ingredients
- 1 medium onion
- 3 pound russet (baking) potatoes (about 6)
- 2 teaspoons fresh lemon juice
- 1/3 cup all-purpose flour
- 3 large eggs, lightly beaten
- About 1 cup vegetable oil for frying
- sour cream for garnishing

Directions
- Cut onion lengthwise to fit feed tube of a food processor, then grate with medium shredding disk.
- Transfer to a large bowl (do not clean processor).
- Peel potatoes and put in a bowl of cold water.
- Spiralize the potatoes and add to onions.
- Toss with lemon juice, then with flour, 2 teaspoons salt, and 1 teaspoon pepper.
- Add eggs and stir to coat.
- Transfer to a colander set over a bowl (potatoes will release juices).
- Preheat oven to 200°F.
- Heat 1/4 inch oil to 360°F in a 12-inch heavy skillet over medium heat.
- Using a 1/4-cup measure, scoop 4 or 5 mounds of potato mixture into skillet.
- Flatten with a fork to form 3 1/2-to 4-inch pancakes.
- Cook until golden brown, 2 1/2 to 3 minutes per side.
- Transfer to a paper-towel-lined baking sheet and keep warm in oven while making more latkes.

Sweet and Breakfast Recipes

Apple Noodles with Cinnamon and Toasted Coconut

Total time: 15 minutes
Servings: 3

Ingredients
- 1 apple per person (I love organic baby Galas)
- coconut oil
- cinnamon, to taste
- unsweetened coconut flakes (enough for a sprinkle on each serving)

Directions
- Spiral slice your apple, using a spiralizer.
- Melt about ½-1 tablespoon of coconut oil in a skillet over medium-high heat. (If you're making multiple apples, add more oil as needed.)
- Sautee your apple noodles in the coconut oil until softened and warmed through.
- Add cinnamon (to taste) and stir to combine.
- Once your apples and cinnamon are finished, remove from skillet and set aside on your serving plate or bowl.
- In the same skillet over medium heat, toss in your unsweetened coconut flakes and allow them to get toasty and brown (keep your eye on them, don't let 'em burn!).
- The flakes will pick up the leftover cinnamon bits and apple juices, making them the perfect topping!

Savoury Parsnip Noodle Chive Waffles (Parsnaffles)

Total time: 25 minutes
Servings: 2 waffles

Ingredients
- ½ tablespoon extra virgin olive oil
- 2 large parsnips, spiralized
- 1/4 teaspoon garlic powder
- salt and pepper, to taste
- 1 large egg, beaten
- 3 tablespoons chopped chives
- optional, to top: ¼ cup greek yogurt, 2 teaspoons lemon juice

Directions
- Preheat a Belgian waffle iron.
- Meanwhile, place a large skillet over medium heat and add in the olive oil.
- Once oil heats, add in the parsnip noodles and season with garlic powder, salt and pepper. Cover and cook for 5 minutes or until noodles are wilted and cooked through.
- Once cooked, add to a bowl with the egg and chives and toss to combine.
- Spray the waffle iron with cooking spray and then pack in the parsnip mixture.
- Cook to the waffle iron's settings and then remove carefully.
- Optional: while waffles are cooking, mix together Greek Yogurt and lemon juice and season with pepper.
- When waffles are done, top with optional Greek yogurt or serve as is, ideally with salty bacon or maple syrup.

Nutritional Information: 1 serving
- 192 calories
- 7g total fat
- 93mg cholesterol
- 8g sugars
- 5g proteins

Sweet Potato Waffles with Pecan Honey Butter

Total time: 35 minutes
Servings: 4

Ingredients
- 1 large sweet potato, spiralized
- 4 eggs
- 1 (13.5) ounce can coconut milk
- 6 tablespoons butter, melted
- 1 teaspoon vanilla extract
- 2 teaspoons baking powder
- 1/4 cup brown sugar
- 2 cups flour
- 1/4 teaspoon nutmeg
- 1/2 teaspoon cinnamon
- 1 teaspoon salt
- 1 stick (or 1/2 cup) butter, room temperature
- 1/2 cup chopped pecans
- 2 tablespoons honey

Directions
- Cook the sweet potato noodles for about 20 minutes.
- While the potatoes are cooking, make the pecan honey butter.
- Combine butter, pecans and honey until fully incorporated.
- Place in refrigerator until ready to use.
- In a blender or food processor combine all of the wet ingredients.
- Drop in cooked sweet potato noodles and blend until smooth.
- Throw in the dry ingredients and blend again until smooth.
- Pour batter into waffle iron and follow the specific instructions for your iron.
- Top with butter, powdered sugar and maple syrup, Enjoy!

Nutritional Information: 1 serving
- 180 calories
- 9g total fat
- 95mg cholesterol
- 6g sugars
- 8g proteins

Apple Whole Wheat Pancakes with Cinnamon Butter

Total time: 25 minutes
Servings: 6

Ingredients
- firm apple
- nonstick cooking spray
- 1 tablespoon cinnamon sugar
- 2 large eggs, separated
- 1 cup low fat buttermilk
- 1 cup low fat milk
- 2 tablespoons oil (canola or safflower)
- 2 tablespoons sugar
- 2 cups whole wheat flour
- 2 teaspoons baking powder
- 1/2 teaspoon baking soda
- 1/2 teaspoon salt

Cinnamon Butter:
- 6 tablespoons butter, softened
- 1 tablespoon cinnamon sugar

Directions
- Preheat griddle to 350°F.

Cinnamon Butter:
- Stir together softened butter and cinnamon sugar in a small bowl.
- Set aside.
- Using a spiralizer, cut apple into thin strands.
- Cut slices into eighths.
- Heat a small skillet over medium heat.
- Spray with nonstick cooking spray.
- Add sliced apple and stir in 1 tablespoon cinnamon sugar.
- Sauté for 10 minutes until apple slices are softened.
- Remove from heat and allow to cool.
- Add egg whites to a bowl and whip until stiff peaks form, about 1 minute.
- Transfer whipped egg whites to a separate bowl.
- Add egg yolks, buttermilk, milk, oil and sugar to mixer bowl.
- Mix until combined.

- In a separate small bowl, combine flour, baking powder, baking soda and salt.
- Fold in apple slices and egg whites.
- Spray griddle with nonstick cooking spray and drop ¼ cup portions of batter onto griddle.
- Flip pancakes when bubbles form on top and bottom is golden brown, about 1 minute.
- Cook for 1- 2 minutes longer on opposite side, or until cooked through.
- Serve with cinnamon butter.

Nutritional Information: 1 serving
- 376 calories
- 41g carbs
- 103mg cholesterol
- 21g fat
- 9g protein
- 91mg sodium

Country Wheat Carrot Cake Muffins with Buttermilk Glaze

Total time: 40 minutes
Servings: 12

Ingredients
- nonstick cooking spray
- 2 - 3 large carrots (2 - inch diameter), peeled and ends trimmed, cut into 4 - inch sections
- 1 1/2 cups all - purpose flour
- 1 cup whole wheat flour
- 2 teaspoons baking powder
- 1/2 teaspoon baking soda
- 1 1/2 teaspoons cinnamon
- ¼ teaspoon nutmeg
- 1/2 teaspoon salt
- 3 large eggs, separated
- ⅓ cup oil (canola or safflower) 1 ⅓ cup low fat buttermilk
- 3/4 cup sugar
- 1 teaspoon vanilla

Buttermilk Glaze:
- 1 cup powdered sugar
- 1/2 teaspoon vanilla
- 2 tablespoons low fat buttermilk

Directions
- Preheat oven to 375°F.
- Spray a 12 - cavity muffin pan with nonstick cooking spray or line with cupcake liners.
- Using a spiralizer, cut the carrot into thin strands.
- Cut sliced carrots in half to form half-circles, it should yield about 1 1/2 cups.
- In a medium bowl, combine all purpose flour, whole wheat flour, baking powder, baking soda, cinnamon, nutmeg and salt.
- Add the egg whites to a bowl and whip until stiff peaks form, about 1 minute.
- Transfer the whipped egg whites to a separate bowl.
- Add egg yolks, oil, buttermilk, sugar and vanilla to mixer bowl.

- Gradually add the dry mixture to the wet mixture, mixing until just combined. Mix in carrots using speed 2.
- Fold in half of the whipped egg whites on stir speed.
- Fold in the remaining half by hand.
- Using prepared muffin pan, fill each cup about 2/3 full.
- Bake for 25 minutes or until an inserted toothpick comes out clean. Remove muffins from pan and cool about 10 minutes.
- Drizzle with glaze while slightly warm.

Buttermilk Glaze:
- Add sugar, vanilla and buttermilk to a bowl and mix for 1 minute or until well combined.
- Scrape down bowl and finish by beating on medium - high for 30 seconds.

Nutritional Information: 1 serving
- 317 calories
- 45g carbs
- 173mg cholesterol
- 12g fat
- 9g protein
- 195mg sodium

Hash Brown Waffles

Total time: 30 minutes
Servings: 2 (7-8" WAFFLE)

Ingredients
- 2 medium russet potatoes, ends trimmed
- 1/2 teaspoon kosher salt
- ¼ teaspoon pepper
- nonstick cooking spray

Directions
- Preheat a waffle maker.
- Using a spiralizer, cut potato into thin strands.
- Repeat with remaining potato to yield 2 1/2 - 3 cups of spiralized potatoes.
- Toss potatoes with salt and pepper.
- Spray the waffle maker liberally with nonstick cooking spray.
- Arrange potatoes on waffle maker and spray potatoes with cooking spray.
- Close lid and press down to compress hash browns.
- Cook for 20 minutes or until the outside of the hash brown is crispy, golden brown and the inside is tender.

Nutritional Information: 1 serving
- 174 calories
- 40g carbs
- 0mg cholesterol
- 1g fat
- 4g protein
- 897mg sodium

Mini Sweet Potato and Spinach Frittatas

Total time: 40 minutes
Servings: 12

Ingredients
- nonstick cooking spray
- 2 medium sweet potatoes, ends trimmed, cut into 4 - inch sections
- 3 tablespoons olive oil, divided
- 3/4 teaspoon salt, divided
- 1/3 cup finely chopped shallot
- 5 ounces baby spinach, roughly chopped
- 5 large eggs
- 1/3 cup low fat milk
- 1/4 teaspoon pepper
- 1 teaspoon italian seasoning
- 3/4 cup crumbled feta cheese
- 1/4 cup grated parmesan cheese

Directions
- Preheat the oven to 375°F.
- Spray a 12 - cavity muffin pan with nonstick cooking spray.
- Using a spiralizer, cut the sweet potato into thin strands.
- Repeat with the remaining sweet potato sections.
- Toss spiralized sweet potatoes with 2 tablespoons oil and 1/4 teaspoon salt in a medium bowl.
- Fit spiralized sweet potatoes into each muffin cavity, dividing evenly.
- Bake in the center of the oven for 20 minutes or until potatoes are just tender.
- While potatoes are baking, heat 1 tablespoon oil in 12 - inch skillet over medium heat.
- Add shallots and stir until softened, about 1- 2 minutes.
- Sprinkle with 1/4 teaspoon salt.
- Add spinach and stir until spinach wilts completely and moisture has evaporated, about 5 minutes.
- Remove from heat.
- Add eggs, milk, remaining 1/4 teaspoon salt, pepper and italian seasoning.

- Whip until well combined and starting to froth.
- Carefully remove the muffin pan from the oven.
- Spray sweet potatoes again with nonstick cooking spray and evenly divide the spinach mixture over roasted sweet potatoes; top evenly with feta cheese.
- Pour egg mixture into each cavity, filling about 2⁄3 full.
- Sprinkle each with parmesan cheese.
- Bake for 17- 20 minutes or until set in the centers and beginning to brown.
- Serve immediately, or cool and store in refrigerator or freezer.
- To warm, preheat oven to 275°F and heat frittatas for 20 minutes or until heated through.

Nutritional Information: 1 serving
- 234 calories
- 7g carbs
- 438mg cholesterol
- 16g fat
- 16g protein
- 431mg sodium

Overnight Zucchini and Turkey Sausage Whole Wheat Egg Strata

Servings: 10 - 12

Ingredients
- 1 pound loaf whole wheat bread (rustic type loaf)
- nonstick cooking spray or butter (to prepare baking sheet)
- 2 medium zucchini, cut into 4 - inch sections, ends trimmed
- 2 tablespoons olive oil, divided
- 12 ounces mild italian turkey sausage
- 1 cup quartered and thinly sliced leek, light green and white parts only
- 1¼ teaspoons kosher salt, divided
- 1 cup chopped roasted red pepper, patted dry
- 2 cups shredded gruyere cheese
- 1 cup grated parmesan cheese
- 11 large eggs
- 2 3/4 cups low fat milk
- 2 tablespoons spicy brown mustard
- ¼ teaspoon pepper
- 2 teaspoons italian seasoning

Directions
- Preheat the oven to 350°F.
- Slice the bread into 3/4 - inch cubes and spread in a single layer on a large sheet pan.
- Bake until dry and toasted, about 15 minutes. Spray a 13 x 9 x 2 - inch baking dish with nonstick cooking spray or grease with butter.
- Using a spiralizer, cut the zucchini into thin strands.
- Repeat with the remaining zucchini to yield about 4 - cups spiralized zucchini.
- Heat 1 tablespoon oil in 12 - inch skillet over medium heat.
- Remove sausage from casing and add bite-sized pieces to skillet.
- Brown sausage in skillet for 5 minutes; breaking up any large pieces.
- Transfer the browned sausage plate.
- Add 1 tablespoon oil to skillet, if needed.

- Add leeks and ¼ teaspoon salt.
- Cook, stirring frequently over medium heat until softened, about 2 minutes.
- Add zucchini to pan, cook, stirring frequently, for 5 minutes or until all liquid has been released and evaporated.
- Remove from heat.
- Spread half the bread cubes in bottom of prepared baking dish.
- Arrange half the sausage, half the zucchini mixture and half the roasted peppers over bread.
- Sprinkle half the Gruyere cheese and half the Parmesan cheese over mixture.
- Add another layer of bread, sausage, zucchini, roasted peppers and Gruyere.
- Reserve the remaining Parmesan until the end.
- Place eggs, milk, mustard, pepper, Italian seasoning and 1 teaspoon salt in bowl.
- Whip on until well combined and starting to froth.
- Pour egg mixture evenly over entire dish.
- Top with remaining Parmesan cheese.
- Cover, refrigerate overnight.
- When ready to bake, place dish, uncovered on large baking sheet.
- Preheat oven to 325°F.
- Bake for 30minutes.
- Raise oven temperature to 350°F.
- Tent dish with foil.
- Bake for 30 - 40 minutes or until center is cooked through.

Nutritional Information: 1 serving
- 426 calories
- 31g carbs
- 285mg cholesterol
- 22g fat
- 28g protein
- 1094mg sodium

Spanish Tortilla Skillet

Total time: 25 minutes
Servings: 4

Ingredients
- 2 medium red potatoes, ends trimmed
- 1 medium sweet potato, cut in half and ends trimmed
- 1 small red onion, peeled, ends trimmed
- 6 large eggs
- 1/2 teaspoon salt
- 1/2 teaspoon freshly ground black pepper
- 8 ounces chorizo, casings removed
- 2 teaspoons olive oil
- 1 clove garlic, minced
- 1 cup packed baby kale

Directions
- Preheat the oven to 375°F.
- Using a spiralizer, cut the potato into thin strands.
- In a medium bowl, whisk together eggs, salt and pepper.
- Set aside.
- Cook chorizo in large ovenproof skillet over medium - high heat 4 - 5 minutes until browned and cooked through, stirring to break up meat.
- Transfer to plate, set aside.
- Wipe out excess grease from skillet.
- Heat olive oil in same skillet over medium heat.
- Add vegetables and garlic; cook 8 -10 minutes or until potatoes are tender.
- Stir in kale; sauté 1- 2 minutes or until beginning to wilt.
- Stir in chorizo; pat mixture into even layer.
- Pour egg mixture evenly into skillet.
- Reduce heat to low; cook 1 minute.
- Transfer the skillet to oven.
- Bake 15 -17 minutes or until eggs are cooked through and edge is lightly browned.
- Loosen edge with spatula; invert onto serving plate.
- Cut into four wedges and serve.

Nutritional Information: 1 serving
- 500 calories
- 28g carbs
- 330mg cholesterol
- 31g fat
- 27g protein
- 1150mg sodium

Zucchini Chocolate Chip Muffins

Total time: 40 minutes
Servings: 12

Ingredients
- 3 cups all - purpose flour
- 1 tablespoon baking powder
- 1 1/2 teaspoon cinnamon
- 1 teaspoon salt
- 1 medium zucchini, ends trimmed and cut into 4 - inch sections
- 1 cup sugar
- 3 large eggs
- 1 cup vegetable oil
- 1 teaspoon vanilla
- 1¼ cup chocolate chips

Directions
- Preheat the oven to 350°F.
- Fill 12 - cavity muffin pan with paper liners.
- Sift flour, baking powder, cinnamon and salt together in a medium bowl.
- Using a spiralizer, cut the zucchini into thin strands.
- Cut spiralized zucchini into 1 1/2 - 2 inch pieces. Yield should be about 2 cups.
- Remove Spiralizer from stand mixer, attach the bowl and the flat beater.
- Add sugar, eggs, vegetable oil and vanilla into the bowl and mix on speed 4 until combined.
- Add flour mixture and mix on speed 6 until just combined.
- Fold in the spiralized zucchini and chocolate chips. The batter will be very thick.
- Divide the batter evenly between muffin cavities.
- Bake 20 - 25 minutes or until tester comes out clean.
- Let cool 10 minutes before removing from the pan and transfering to a cooling rack. Continue cooling 1 hour before serving.

Nutritional Information: 1 serving
- 489 calories
- 56g carbs
- 55mg cholesterol
- 27g fat
- 6g protein
- 339mg sodium

Dessert Recipes

Apple Clafouti

Total time: 35 minutes
Servings: 10

Ingredients
- 9 tablespoons butter, softened, divided
- 1 cup heavy cream
- 3 large eggs
- 1 teaspoon vanilla
- 1 teaspoon
- 2⁄3 cup all - purpose flour
- 1 cup sugar, divided
- 1/2 teaspoon salt
- 3 medium tart apples
- 1 teaspoon fresh lemon juice
- 3 tablespoons brandy
- 1/2 teaspoon ground cinnamon

Directions
- Preheat the oven to 400°F.
- Prepare a 9-inch baking pan with 1 tablespoon butter.
- Place the prepared pan in the oven to preheat 10 minutes before baking.
- To make the batter, add cream, eggs, 6 tablespoons butter, flour, 1/2 cup sugar, vanilla and salt in a mixer bowl.
- Whip for about 30 seconds or until combined. Set the bowl aside.
- Using a spiralizer, cut the apples into thin strands.
- Stand sliced apples on end and cut in half to make half circles; place in a medium bowl.
- Add lemon juice; toss to coat.
- Melt remaining 2 tablespoons butter in medium skillet over medium - high heat.
- Add apples and remaining 1/2 cup sugar; sauté 2 minutes.
- Add brandy; sauté 2 minutes.

- Transfer apple mixture to medium bowl with slotted spoon, leaving juices in skillet.
- Pour half of batter into hot baking dish.
- Arrange apple mixture over batter; top with remaining batter and sprinkle with cinnamon.
- Bake 18 - 20 minutes or until edge is golden and center is set.
- Let cool slightly.
- If desired, warm skillet drippings and drizzle over clafouti.

Nutritional Information: 1 serving
- 350 calories
- 38g carbs
- 115mg cholesterol
- 20g fat
- 4g protein
- 150mg sodium

Apple and Cranberry Tart with Whole Wheat Crust

Total time: 1 hour 20 minutes
Servings: 8 - 10

Ingredients
- 1/2 cup walnuts
- 1 1/3 cups whole wheat flour
- 1/2 teaspoon salt
- 1/3 cup sugar
- 1/3 cup oil (canola or safflower)
- 1 tablespoon cold water

Tart filling:
- 3 firm apples (green or red)
- 1/3 cup packed light brown sugar
- 2 tablespoons all purpose flour
- 1/2 teaspoon cinnamon
- 1/8 teaspoon salt
- ¼ cup apple jelly
- ¼ cup dried cranberries

Directions
- Preheat the oven to 375°F.
- Pulse the walnuts in a food processor until they are finely ground.
- Add the flour, salt and sugar.
- Pulse 2 - 3 times to combine. While processor is running, drizzle in 1/3 cup oil.
- Sprinkle water over the mixture and pulse 2 - 3 times to combine.
- Press the crust mixture evenly into the bottom of an 1 1 1/2 - inch tart pan with a removable bottom.
- Place the tart pan on a large baking sheet and bake 20 minutes or until the walnuts become fragrant.
- Using a spiralizer, cut the apples into thin strands.
- Stand sliced apples on end and cut in half to make half cirlces.
- Combine brown sugar, flour, cinnamon and salt in a medium bowl.
- Add apple slices and gently toss to coat.

- Arrange one layer of overlapping apple slices around bottom perimeter of baked crust.
- Arrange additional apple slices in a single layer, filling in the center of apple ring.
- Continue with additional layers until pan is full.
- Bake for 25 - 30 minutes or until the apples are tender.
- In small microwave - safe bowl, combine apple jelly and cranberries.
- Microwave for 30 - 40 seconds or until the jelly starts to bubble.
- Remove and stir until completely melted.
- Spoon melted jelly and cranberries evenly over apples.
- Use a pastry brush to evenly coat apples.
- Allow to rest 10 minutes before serving.

Nutritional Information: 1 serving
- 287 calories
- 46g carbs
- 0mg cholesterol
- 12g fat
- 4g protein
- 6mg sodium

Chocolate Beet Cake

Total time: 35 minutes
Servings: 10

Ingredients
- Nonstick cooking spray or butter for greasing
- 2 medium beets, scrubbed and ends trimmed
- 1¼ cups all purpose flour
- 3 tablespoons unsweetened cocoa powder
- 1 1/2 teaspoons baking powder
- 1/2 teaspoon salt
- 3 eggs, separated
- 1 cup sugar
- 8 ounces bittersweet chocolate, chopped
- ¼ cup hot strong brewed coffee or espresso
- whipped cream and shaved chocolate (optional)

Directions
- Preheat the oven to 375°F
- Prepare an 8 - or 9 - inch spring form pan by greasing with butter or nonstick cooking spray.
- Using a spiralizer, cut the beet into thin strands.
- Spread the beets on a large baking sheet.
- Bake 15 - 20 minutes or until beets are fork tender. Cool completely.
- Cut into ¼ - inch pieces.
- Reduce the oven temperature to 325°F.
- Sift flour, cocoa, baking powder and salt into a small bowl.
- Add the egg whites in a bowl and whip until soft peaks form.
- Gradually add the sugar, whipping until mixture is glossy and stiff peaks form.
- Melt the chocolate in a small saucepan over low heat, stirring constantly until smooth.
- Stir in coffee until well blended.
- Transfer mixture to a large bowl.
- Stir in egg yolks one at a time.
- Stir in beets.
- Fold in egg whites, then fold in flour mixture.
- Pour batter evenly into prepared pan and smooth top.

- Bake 40 - 45 minutes or until toothpick inserted into center comes out with moist crumbs.
- Cool completely in the pan on a wire rack.
- Run a knife around the edge of the pan to loosen cake.
- Remove the side of the pan. Serve with whipped cream and shaved chocolate, if desired.
- *NOTE: This cake is best served the day it is made.

Nutritional Information: 1 serving
- 290 calories
- 49g carbs
- 75mg cholesterol
- 9g fat
- 5g protein
- 240mg sodium

Chocolate Zucchini Cake with Chocolate - Hazelnut Swirl

Total time: 40 minutes
Servings: 24

Ingredients
- nonstick cooking spray
- 2 medium zucchini, ends trimmed, cut into 4 - inch sections
- 2¼ cups cake flour
- ⅓ cup unsweetened cocoa powder
- 1 teaspoon baking soda
- 1 teaspoon salt
- 1 1/2 cups sugar
- 3/4 cup butter, softened
- 2 large eggs
- 1 teaspoon vanilla
- ⅔ cup buttermilk
- 1 cup bittersweet chocolate chips
- 1/2 cup chocolate-hazelnut spread

Directions
- Preheat the oven to 325°F.
- Prepare a 9 x13 - inch baking pan with nonstick cooking spray.
- Using a spiralizer, cut the zucchini into thin strands.
- Coarsely chop the spiralized zucchini.
- In a separate medium bowl, sift the flour, cocoa powder, baking soda and salt together, stir to combine.
- Add butter and sugar into mixer bowl; beat on speed 4 for 3 - 5 minutes or until light and fluffy.
- Add eggs, one at a time, mixing well after each egg.
- Mix in vanilla.
- Add flour mixture alternately with buttermilk, mixing on speed 2 after each addition.
- Gently fold in chopped zucchini and chocolate chips.
- Pour mixture evenly into prepared pan.
- Microwave chocolate - hazelnut spread in a small microwave safe bowl, 10 -15 seconds or until softened.

- Drop spoonfuls of the spread onto the batter; swirl into batter with knife.
- Bake 45 - 50 minutes or until toothpick inserted into center comes out clean.
- Cool completely in pan on wire rack. Cut into squares to serve.

Nutritional Information: 1 serving
- 230 calories
- 31g carbs
- 30mg cholesterol
- 11g fat
- 3g protein
- 170mg sodium

Free Form Apple Tart

Total time: 1 hour
Servings: 6

Ingredients
- 2¼ cups all - purpose flour
- 1/2 teaspoon kosher salt
- 11/2 sticks butter, cut into small pieces
- 6-8 tablespoons ice water
- 6 tart apples
- ⅓ cup sugar
- 1/2 teaspoon cinnamon
- 1/2 teaspoon lemon juice
- ¼ teaspoon salt
- 1 egg white
- raw sugar

Directions
- Preheat the oven to 400°F.
- Measure the flour and salt into a mixer bowl; mix for 10 seconds or until combined.
- Add the butter and mix on speed 2 for 1- 2 minutes or until mixture resembles coarse crumbs.
- Add ice water, 1 tablespoon at a time, until the dough holds together.
- Remove from bowl and place onto floured surface.
- Roll out dough to a 16 - inch round and transfer to large baking sheet.
- Using a spiralizer, cut apples into thin strands.
- Cut each sliced apple in half to make half circles.
- Arrange apple slices in a spiral pattern in center of pastry, leaving 3 - inch border all around.
- Combine sugar, cinnamon, and lemon juice in small bowl.
- Sprinkle evenly over apples.
- Fold edges of dough up around apples.
- Brush with egg white and sprinkle with raw sugar.
- Bake in the preheated oven for 40 - 50 minutes or until pastry is brown and apples are tender.
- Transfer to a cooling rack.

- Cool slightly before cutting into 6 wedges for serving.

Nutritional Information: 1 serving
- 523 calories
- 75g carbs
- 61mg cholesterol
- 24g fat
- 6g protein
- 463mg sodium

Pear Crisp

Total time: 1 hour
Servings: 6

Ingredients
- nonstick cooking spray
- 1/2 cup whole almonds
- 1 cup all purpose flour
- 1 cup old-fashioned oats
- 3/4 cup packed brown sugar
- 1/2 teaspoon salt
- 1/2 cup cold butter, cut into cubes
- 4 d'anjou pears, ends trimmed
- 1 teaspoon fresh lemon juice
- 1/2 teaspoon grated fresh ginger
- ice cream or whipped cream (optional)

Directions
- Preheat the oven to 375°F.
- Prepare a 9 - inch square baking pan with nonstick cooking spray.
- Place almonds in a Food Processor; pulse about 15 times or until coarsely chopped.
- Add flour, oats, brown sugar and salt; break up brown sugar with wooden spoon.
- Pulse 5 times to combine.
- Add butter; pulse until mixture forms coarse crumbs.
- Using a spiralizer, cut the pears into thin strands.
- Arrange the sliced pears in prepared baking pan.
- Combine lemon juice and ginger in small bowl; brush evenly over pears.
- Sprinkle with crumb mixture.
- Bake 40 - 45 minutes or until topping is golden brown and pears are tender.
- Cool slightly.
- Serve with ice cream or whipped cream, if desired.

Nutritional Information: 1 serving
- 380 calories
- 54g carbs
- 30mg cholesterol
- 17g fat
- 5g protein
- 160mg sodium

Plantain Truffles

Total time: 35 minutes
Servings: 10(20 truffles)

- **Ingredients**
- 2 firm plantains, peeled and cut into 4 - inch sections
- 6 pitted dried dates
- 1/2 cup hot water
- 2 tablespoons coconut oil
- 2/3 cup sweetened flaked coconut
- ¼ cup unsweetened cocoa powder
- 2 tablespoons agave nectar
- 1/2 teaspoon salt
- 1/2 teaspoon vanilla

Directions
- Line a large baking sheet with parchment paper.
- Using a spiralizer, cut the plantain into thin strands.
- Place sliced plantains into a Food Processor.
- Pulse 10 times, or until plantains are finely chopped and resemble rice.
- Set aside.
- Place the dates in a small bowl and cover with 1/2 cup hot water.
- Let stand 10 minutes.
- Drain dates, reserving 2 tablespoons of the water.
- Heat the coconut oil in a large nonstick skillet over medium heat.
- Add plantains and sauté about 10 minutes or until golden.
- Let cool 10 minutes.
- Combine the plantains, dates, reserved date water, coconut, cocoa, agave, salt and vanilla in a food processor.
- Pulse 6 - 8 times or until combined.
- Shape tablespoons of mixture into 1- inch balls.
- Roll truffles in pistachios, additional cocoa or flaked coconut, if desired, and place on prepared baking sheet.
- Store in refrigerator.

Nutritional Information: 1 serving
- 170 calories
- 33g carbs
- 0mg cholesterol
- 5g fat
- 2g protein
- 135mg sodium

Upside Down Pineapple Cake

Total time: 40 minutes
Servings: 8

Ingredients
- 1 pineapple, cut in half crosswise, skin removed
- 1¼ cups (2 1/2 sticks) butter, softened, divided
- 1 teaspoon honey
- 1 teaspoon dark rum
- ⅓ cup packed brown sugar
- 1/2 teaspoon plus
- ⅛ teaspoon salt, divided
- 1/2 cup granulated sugar
- 2 large eggs
- 1 tablespoon milk
- 1/2 teaspoon vanilla
- 1 ⅓ cups all - purpose flour
- 2 teaspoons baking powder

Directions
- Preheat the oven to 350°F.
- Using a spiralizer, cut the pineapple into thin strands.
- Place the sliced pineapples on paper towel lined surface to absorb excess moisture.
- Add ¼ cup butter, brown sugar, honey, rum and ⅛ teaspoon salt in mixer bowl; mix until smooth.
- Spread evenly into 9 - inch round cake pan.
- Arrange the pineapple slices evenly over the butter mixture.
- Add remaining 1 cup butter to mixer bowl; mix on speed 4 until creamy.
- Add granulated sugar; mix for 3 - 4 minutes or until fluffy.
- Add eggs, milk and vanilla; mix until combined.
- Add flour, baking powder and remaining 1/2 teaspoon salt; mix for about 30 seconds or just until combined.
- Spread batter over pineapple slices with spatula or clean, dampened fingers.
- Bake 30 - 35 minutes or until toothpick inserted into center comes out clean.
- Cool in pan on wire rack 15 minutes.

- Run thin knife around edge of pan to loosen cake.
- Place serving plate over pan; invert cake onto serving plate.

Nutritional Information: 1 serving
- 490 calories
- 53g carbs
- 125mg cholesterol
- 30g fat
- 5g protein
- 310mg sodium

Whole Wheat Pear and Apple Crisp

Total time: 1 hour
Servings: 6 - 8

- **Ingredients**
- nonstick cooking spray
- 6 tablespoons unsalted butter, cut into tablespoon pieces
- 2/3 cup light brown sugar
- ¼ cup whole wheat flour
- 2 tablespoons toasted wheat germ
- ¼ teaspoon salt
- 1/2 teaspoon cinnamon
- ¼ teaspoon nutmeg
- 1/2 cup old-fashioned oats
- 1 green apple
- 1 red apple
- 2 firm pears
- ¼ cup water
- 1 tablespoon cornstarch
- whipped cream (optional)
- ice cream (optional)

Directions
- Preheat the oven to 350°F.
- Prepare an 8 x 8 x 2 - inch baking pan with nonstick cooking spray or coat pan with additional butter.
- Add butter, brown sugar, flour, wheat germ, salt, cinnamon and nutmeg in a mixing bowl.
- Mix until crumbly, about 1 minute. Stir in oatmeal. Set aside.
- Using a spiralizer, cut apples into thin strands.
- Repeat with remaining apple and pears.
- Cut sliced fruit into quarters and add to prepared baking pan.
- Toss to combine apple and pear slices.
- In a small bowl, whisk together water and cornstarch.
- Pour over sliced apples and pears, and top evenly with crumb topping.
- Bake 40 minutes, or until fruit is bubbly and topping is lightly browned.

- Let rest for 15 minutes before serving.
- Serve with whipped cream or ice cream, if desired.

Nutritional Information: 1 serving
- 284 calories
- 47g carbs
- 26mg cholesterol
- 11g fat
- 3g protein
- 160mg sodium

Soup Recipes

Kale and Butternut Squash Noodle Soup

Total time: 30 minutes
Servings: 6

Ingredients
- 1 yellow onion, chopped
- ½ tablespoon extra virgin olive oil
- ½ of 34 oz can of whole, peeled tomatoes
- 1 garlic clove
- 6 cups low-sodium vegetable broth
- 2 stalks celery
- ½ teaspoon freshly ground black pepper (more to taste)
- ½ teaspoon oregano
- ½ teaspoon no-salt spice blend (like Mrs. Dash)
- ¼ teaspoon chili powder
- 1 butternut squash*, spiralized or chopped
- 1 large bunch kale (the more the greener!)
- 1 cup white cannelloni beans, rinsed and drained if from a can
- 2 teaspoons fresh chives, chopped
Optional: Garnish with parmesan cheese and additional chives

Directions
- In a large stock pot, heat oil over medium heat.
- Once oil is hot, add onions.
- Stir continuously until translucent.
- Add tomatoes, garlic [whole], broth, and celery.
- Mix well, chopping the tomatoes with a wooden spoon.
- Bring soup to a boil, then reduce to a simmer and add spices. Stir to combine.
- If serving immediately, add butternut squash, kale, white beans, and chives.
- Cover and let continue to simmer on low heat for 20 minutes.
- If making hours to a day before serving, cover the broth and let simmer for 20 minutes (you will add the remaining ingredients when reheating).

- Turn off the heat and add additional kale before serving.
- Top with chives and parmesan cheese, if desired.
- Enjoy!

*Note: If spiralizing the butternut squash, keep in mind that the noodles will cook much faster than if chopped. If not serving immediately, add the butternut squash noodles when letting soup simmer or when re-heating the soup.

Asian Noodle Soup

Total time: 40 minutes
Servings: 4

Ingredients
- 1 small onion, peeled and ends trimmed
- 2 medium zucchini, ends trimmed and cut into 4 - inch sections
- 2 tablespoons oil, divided (canola or safflower)
- 4 ounces shiitake mushrooms, thinly sliced
- 1 teaspoon minced fresh garlic
- 2 teaspoons fresh ginger, peeled and finely grated
- 1/2 teaspoon Chinese 5-spice powder
- 6 cups low sodium chicken broth
- ¼ cup soy sauce
- 2 eggs, lightly beaten
- 2 tablespoons chopped cilantro
- 1 tablespoon lime juice
- 1/2 teaspoon salt

Toppings:
- Fresh basil
- Fresh mint
- Fresh cilantro
- Lime wedges
- Sriracha chile sauce
- Fresh mung bean sprouts

Directions
- Using a spiralizer, cut onion into thin strands.
- Yield about 1/2 cup spiralized oinion.
- Repeat with zucchini sections.
- Yields about 6 cups spiralized zucchini.
- Cut spiralized vegetables into 2 - inch pieces.
- Heat oil over medium heat in large stock pot.
- Add mushroom and onion, cook, stirring occasionally for 5 minutes or until softened and beginning to brown.
- Add garlic, ginger and 5 - spice powder, stir for 30 seconds.
- Add broth and soy sauce, bring to a simmer.
- Reduce heat and simmer for 20 minutes.

- When almost ready to serve, stir soup continuously while drizzling beaten eggs into soup in a thin stream.
- Add cilantro and lime juice.
- Heat a large 12 - inch skillet over medium heat, add 1 tablespoon oil and zucchini noodles.
- Sprinkle with salt.
- Cook while tossing with tongs for 2 - 3 minutes or until slightly softened and just starting to release some juices.
- Divide sliced zucchini evenly into 4 bowls and top with soup.
- Serve with toppings.

Nutritional Information: 1 serving
- 207 calories
- 17g carbs
- 106mg cholesterol
- 12g fat
- 13g protein
- 911mg sodium

Minestrone Soup

Total time: 1 hour
Servings: 6 - 8

Ingredients
- 1 small onion, peeled, ends trimmed
- 1 large fennel bulb, ends trimmed, reserve fronds
- 2 large carrots, peeled and ends trimmed, cut into 4 - inch sections
- 1 large zucchini, ends trimmed, cut into 4 - inch sections
- 2 tablespoons olive oil, divided
- 12 ounces mild italian turkey sausage
- 1 teaspoon minced fresh garlic
- 1 teaspoon fresh thyme leaves
- 1/2 teaspoon minced fresh rosemary
- ¼ teaspoon pepper
- 1-14.5 ounce can petite - diced tomatoes
- 10 cups low sodium chicken broth
- 1-15.5 ounce can cannellini beans, drained and rinsed
- ¼ cup chopped flat leaf parsley
- 1 tablespoon minced fennel fronds
- 1/2 teaspoon kosher salt (optional)
- Parmesan cheese for topping

Directions
- Using a spiralizer, cut onions into thin strands.
- Repeat with fennel, carrots and zucchini into same bowl.
- Cut spiralized vegetables to desired length.
- Set aside.
- In a large stock pot, 5 quarts or more, heat oil over medium heat.
- Remove sausage from casing and cut into bite sized pieces, add to pot.
- Brown sausage for 5 minutes.
- Transfer browned sausage to plate; set aside.
- Add additional 1 tablespoon oil to pot if needed.
- Add spiralized onion, fennel, carrot and garlic to pot, stirring constantly for 3 minutes.

- Add thyme, rosemary, pepper and tomatoes to pot, continue stirring.
- Scrape up any browned bits from bottom of pot.
- Add sausage back to pot.
- Pour in broth, add beans.
- Bring to boil over medium heat.
- Reduce heat to low, cover pot and cook 30 minutes, stirring occasionally.
- Add zucchini, parsley and fennel fronds.
- Simmer until zucchini is tender, about 10 minutes.
- Add salt to taste.
- Divide soup evenly into 6 - 8 bowls, top with Parmesan cheese if desired.

Nutritional Information: 1 serving
- 249 calories
- 19g carbs
- 41mg cholesterol
- 11g fat
- 22g protein
- 472mg sodium

Simple Chicken Soup with Zucchini Noodles

Total time: 40 minutes
Servings: 6

Ingredients
- 2 teaspoons olive oil
- 1 small onion, peeled and chopped
- 2 stalks celery, chopped
- 3 carrots, peeled and chopped
- 1 clove garlic, minced
- 8 cups chicken broth
- 1 teaspoon minced fresh thyme or 1/2 teaspoon dried thyme
- 2 medium zucchini, cut into 4 - inch sections, ends trimmed
- 1/2 rotisserie chicken, cut into bite-size pieces (about 1 cup)
- salt and freshly ground black pepper

Directions
- Heat 2 teaspoons olive oil in large saucepan or stockpot.
- Add onion, celery, carrots and garlic; sauté 5 minutes or until onion is translucent and vegetables are softened.
- Add broth and thyme.
- Bring to boil over high heat.
- Reduce heat to medium - low; simmer 20 minutes.
- Using a spiralizer, cut zucchini into thin strands.
- Cut spiralized zucchini to desired length.
- Add chicken to soup; cook 5 minutes.
- Add zucchini noodles; cook 1- 2 minutes or until softened.
- Divide soup evenly into 6 bowls and serve.

Nutritional Information: 1 serving
- 210 calories
- 19g carbs
- 30mg cholesterol
- 7g fat
- 16g protein
- 520mg sodium

Spicy Greens and Zucchini Noodle Soup

Total time: 50 minutes
Servings: 4

Ingredients
- 1 pound ground pork
- 4 cloves garlic, minced
- 2 teaspoons minced ginger
- 1/2 teaspoon dry mustard
- 1/2 teaspoon ground coriander
- 1 teaspoon ground cumin
- 1 teaspoons black peppercorns, coarsely ground
- 1 teaspoon pink peppercorns, coarsely ground
- 3 teaspoons olive oil, divided
- 6 cups vegetable stock
- 1 teaspoon fish sauce
- 6 cups greens (kale, mustard, dandelion or a combination)
- 1/2 cup snap peas
- 3 medium zucchini, cut into 4 - inch sections, ends trimmed

Directions
- Preheat the oven to 350°F.
- Combine pork, garlic, ginger, mustard, coriander, cumin and peppercorns in large bowl.
- Heat 2 teaspoons olive oil in large saucepan over medium heat.
- Add pork mixture; cook 10 minutes or until pork is no longer pink, stirring to break up meat.
- Add broth and fish sauce. Bring to simmer over medium - high heat.
- Reduce heat to medium - low; simmer 20 minutes.
- Add greens and peas; cook 4 minutes or until greens are wilted.
- Using a spiralizer, cut zucchini into thin strands.
- Toss spiralized zucchini with remaining teaspoon olive oil.
- Spread zucchini onto 9 x13 - inch baking pan.
- Bake 7 -10 minutes or until zucchini is tender.
- Divide zucchini among 4 bowls, top with soup, and serve.

Nutritional Information: 1 serving

- 465 calories
- 21g carbs
- 74mg cholesterol
- 30g fat
- 33g protein
- 339mg sodium

Zucchini and Daikon Ramen with Pork

Total time: 40 minutes
Servings: 4

Ingredients
- 2 medium zucchini, cut into 4 – inch sections, ends trimmed
- 1 medium daikon radish (about 6 - inches), cut in half, ends trimmed
- 2 teaspoons vegetable oil
- 6 cups chicken broth
- 2 tablespoons mirin
- 2 tablespoons miso paste
- 2 teaspoons dark sesame oil
- 1 cup packed baby spinach
- 4 large eggs
- 1 cup shiitake mushrooms,stems removed
- 1 jalapeño pepper, seeded and thinly sliced
- ¼ cup chopped fresh cilantro
- ¼ cup shredded fresh basil

Pork marinade:
- ¼ cup chopped green onion
- ¼ cup unseasoned rice vinegar
- ¼ cup soy sauce, divided
- 1 tablespoon honey
- 1 tablespoon sriracha sauce
- 5 cloves garlic, minced, divided
- 1 teaspoon minced fresh ginger
- 1 pork tenderloin (about 1 pound)

Directions
- Preheat the oven TO 400°F.

Pork marinade:
- Combine green onions, vinegar, 2 tablespoons soysauce, honey, sriracha, 3 cloves garlic and ginger in small bowl.
- Place pork in large resealable food storage bag; pour marinade over pork.
- Seal bag; marinate in refrigerator at least 2 hours or overnight.
- Drain pork, discard marinade.

- Place marinated pork on baking pan.
- Bake 25 - 30 minutes or until pork reaches 145°F.
- Transfer to cutting board; set aside.
- Heat vegetable oil in large saucepan over medium - high heat.
- Add remaining 2 cloves garlic; sauté 1 minute.
- Add broth, mirin, miso, remaining 2 tablespoons soy sauce and sesame oil.
- Bring to boil.
- Reduce heat to medium - low; simmer 15 - 20 minutes.
- Place eggs in small saucepan; cover with water.
- Cover, bring to boil over high heat.
- Remove from heat.
- Let stand, covered, 4 minutes.
- Run eggs under cold water until cool enough to handle.
- Peel eggs.
- Using a spiralizer, cut zucchini into thin strands.
- Repeat with remaining zucchini and daikon radish.
- Slice pork into 1/2 - inch slices.
- Divide mushrooms, zucchini, daikon and spinach evenly between 4 bowls.
- Pour about 11/2 cups broth over each serving; let stand 5 minutes.
- Top with 4 - 5 slices of pork and one egg; carefully cut egg in half.
- Top with jalapeño slices, cilantro and basil.
- Serve immediately.

Nutritional Information: 1 serving
- 400 calories
- 28g carbs
- 260mg cholesterol
- 15g fat
- 37g protein
- 3470mg sodium

Zucchini Noodle Wedding Soup

Total time: 30 minutes
Servings: 6

Ingredients
- 2 tablespoons finely minced onion
- 1/2 teaspoon minced fresh garlic
- 1 tablespoon grated parmesan cheese, plus more for serving
- 2 tablespoons milk
- ¼ cup panko bread crumbs
- 1/2 teaspoon dried italian seasoning
- 1 large egg yolk
- 1/2 teaspoon kosher salt, divided
- ¼ teaspoon pepper
- 1/2 teaspoon Worcestershire sauce
- 1/2 pound lean ground beef or turkey
- 3 tablespoons olive oil, divided

Soup ingredients:
- 1/2 cup finely chopped onion
- 1/2 teaspoon minced fresh garlic
- 1 teaspoon fresh thyme leaves
- 1 bay leaf
- 1/2 teaspoon pepper, divided
- 1-14.5 ounce can petite - diced tomatoes
- 8 cups low sodium chicken broth
- 4 cups baby spinach
- 2 large zucchini, cut into 4 - inch sections, ends trimmed

Directions
- In a mixer, place all meatball ingredients, except meat and olive oil, in a bowl and mix until combined.
- Add meat and mix until just combined.
- Scoop 1 teaspoon portions and roll meatballs.
- Heat large stock pot over medium heat, add 2 tablespoons oil.
- Cook meatballs, turning carefully with spatula until browned on all sides, about 6 minutes.
- Cook in batches if necessary.
- Remove meatballs to a platter.

- In the same pot, sauté onions over medium heat, 4 minutes or until translucent.
- Add garlic, thyme, bay leaf, ¼ teaspoon pepper and cook for 1 minute.
- Add tomatoes to pot and stir scraping up any browned bits.
- Add broth and meatballs back to pot and reduce heat, maintain low simmer for 20 minutes or until ready to eat.
- Using a spiralizer, cut zucchini into thin strands.
- Cut spiralized zucchini to desired length.
- When almost ready to serve, stir spinach into soup.
- Heat large 12 - inch skillet over medium heat, add 1 tablespoon olive oil.
- Add spiralized zucchini and sprinkle with salt and pepper.
- Cook and toss spiralized zucchini for 2 - 3 minutes or until slightly softened and just starting to release juices.
- Divide zucchini evenly among 6 bowls and top with soup.
- If desired, sprinkle with Parmesan cheese and parsley.

Nutritional Information: 1 serving
- 234 calories
- 15g carbs
- 66mg cholesterol
- 13g fat
- 17g protein
- 444mg sodium

Appetizer Recipes

Autumn Apple Sangria

Total time: 15 minutes
Servings: 6 (12-OZ) servings

Ingredients
- 4 cups apple cider
- 3 cinnamon sticks
- 1 tablespoon cloves
- Peel from 1/2 orange
- 1 firm apple
- 1 bottle (750 ml) pinot grigio wine
- 1 cup spiced rum
- 24 ounces ginger beer

Optional Garnish: Cinnamon, sugar, orange

Directions
- Combine apple cider, cinnamon sticks, cloves and orange zest in a 2 - quart saucepan and simmer over medium heat until reduced by one - third, about 20 minutes.
- Strain and allow to cool.
- Using a spiralizer, cut apple into thin strands.
- Cut sliced apple into eighths and add to large 3 - quart pitcher.
- Add wine and rum, stir in cooled cider mixture.
- Refrigerate for 4 - 48 hours.
- Serve in 14 - ounce glasses.
- If desired, rub rims of glasses with an orange wedge and dip into cinnamon sugar.
- Fill each glass with 8 - ounces of apple sangria.
- Top each with 4-ounces of ginger beer.
- Garnish with orange slices.

Nutritional Information: 1 serving

- 323 calories
- 36g carbs
- 0mg cholesterol
- 0g fat
- 0g protein
- 16mg sodium

Baked Herbed Spiral Fries with Roasted Red Pepper Dip

Total time: 30 minutes
Servings: 4

Ingredients
- nonstick cooking spray
- 2 large russet potatoes (2 pounds total), ends trimmed
- 1 teaspoon kosher salt, divided
- 1/2 teaspoon pepper
- 2 teaspoons minced fresh thyme
- 1 teaspoon minced fresh rosemary
- 3 tablespoons oil (canola or safflower)

Roasted Red Pepper Dip:
- 4 ounces reduced fat cream cheese
- 1/4 cup light mayonnaise
- 1/2 cup chopped roasted red peppers
- 1/4 teaspoon minced fresh garlic
- 1 tablespoon lemon juice
- 1/4 teaspoon Worcestershire sauce 1/4 teaspoon kosher salt
- 1/4 teaspoon pepper

Directions
- Preheat the over to 425F.
- Arrange 2 oven racks to upper third and lower third positions.
- Line 2 large baking pans with parchment paper or spray with nonstick cooking spray.
- Using a spiralizer, cut potato into thin strands.
- Cut spirals into 7 - 8 sections, place in a large bowl.
- In a small bowl, mix together 1/2 teaspoon salt, pepper, thyme and rosemary.
- Drizzle potatoes with oil, sprinkle with the salt herb mixture and toss well.
- Arrange spirals on prepared baking pans, make sure they are stretched out and standing up. Sprinkle with remaining salt.
- Bake for 10 minutes, rotate pans once while cooking.
- Open oven and use tongs to turn the spirals.

- Repeat process every 10 minutes for a total of 30 minutes, or until potatoes are browned and crispy on the outside, and tender on the inside.

Roasted rep pepper dip:

- Combine all dip ingredients in a mixer bowl, mix until smooth.
- Serve spiral fries immediately with roasted red pepper dip.

Nutritional Information: 1 serving

- 346 calories
- 40g carbs
- 20mg cholesterol
- 20g fat
- 6g protein
- 1210mg sodium

Baked Sweet Potato Chips with Chipotle Lime Aioli

Total time: 1 hour 20 minutes
Servings: 2

Ingredients
- 2 medium sweet potatoes, cut into
- 4 - inch sections, ends trimmed
- 3 tablespoons oil, divided (canola or safflower)
- 1/2 teaspoon ground cumin
- 1/8 teaspoon chipotle chili powder 1/2 teaspoon kosher salt
- ¼ teaspoon pepper

Chipotle Lime Aioli:
- 1 cup light mayonnaise
- 21/2 teaspoons minced chipotles in adobo
- zest of 1/2 lime
- 1 tablespoon lime juice

Directions
- Preheat the oven to 400°F.
- Using a spiralizer, cut the sweet potato into thin strands.
- Soak sweet potatoes in a bowl of cold water for 1 hour to remove some starch. Drain bowl.
- Rinse sweet potato slices and spread onto a clean kitchen towel. Pat tops dry.
- Prepare 2 large baking pans with 1 teaspoon of oil each.
- Spread oil around sheet with paper towel.
- Place pans in oven to preheat.
- Combine cumin, chili powder, salt and pepper in small bowl.
- Set aside.
- Place sweet potato slices in a large bowl.
- Drizzle with 2 tablespoons oil and sprinkle with spice mixture.
- Toss to coat evenly.
- Remove preheated pans, one at a time, from oven and arrange half of potato slices in a single layer on each.
- Return pans to oven.
- Bake for 10 minutes, rotating pans once while cooking.
- Remove from oven and use spatula to flip all chips.

- Bake another 8 -10 minutes, or until sweet potatoes are well browned, rotating pans once while baking.

Chipotle Lime Aioli:
- Combine aioli ingredients in a small bowl and mix together.
- Refrigerate until ready to use.
- Serve chips with chipotle lime aioli.

Nutritional Information: 1 serving
- 349 calories
- 19g carbs
- 21mg cholesterol
- 31g fat
- 2g protein
- 851mg sodium

Focaccia with Squash and Olives

Total time: 40 minutes
Servings: 1 loaf, 12 servings

Ingredients
- 1 packet (¼ ounce) active dry yeast
- 1 cup warm water - 105° to 110°F
- 1 tablespoon sugar
- 3 cups all purpose flour
- ¼ cup extra virgin olive oil
- 1 1/2 teaspoons kosher salt
- 1/2 cup mixed olives
- 1 small zucchini, ends trimmed, cut into 4 - inch sections
- 1 small summer squash, ends trimmed, cut into 4 - inch sections
- 2⁄3 cup shredded parmesan cheese
- 1 teaspoon dried oregano
- 1 tablespoon cornmeal
- 1/2 teaspoon freshly ground black pepper

Directions
- Preheat the oven to 425°F.
- In a mixer, combine water, sugar and yeast in mixer bowl; stir to dissolve yeast.
- Let stand 5 minutes.
- Add flour, olive oil and salt; knead on speed 2 for 3 - 4 minutes or until dough is smooth and elastic.
- Shape dough into a ball.
- Place in large, lightly greased bowl; turn once to grease surface.
- Cover and let rise in warm place about 1 hour or until doubled.
- Grease 9 x13 - inch baking pan; dust with cornmeal.
- Punch down dough; shape into 9 x13 - inch rectangle on lightly floured surface.
- Press lightly into prepared pan.
- Cover and let rise 30 minutes.
- Using a spiralizer, cut zucchini into thin strands.
- Dimple dough all over with fingers.

- Sprinkle cheese evenly over dough; top with zucchini, summer squash and olives.
- Sprinkle with oregano and pepper.
- Bake 25 minutes or until edges are golden.
- Let cool slightly before serving.

Nutritional Information: 1 serving
- 194 calories
- 28g carbs
- 4mg cholesterol
- 7g fat
- 6g protein
- 405mg sodium

Pear Ricotta Toasts

Total time: 10 minutes
Servings: 2

Ingredients
- anjou pear, ends trimmed
- 2 slices sourdough bread, toasted
- 2 tablespoons ricotta cheese
- 1 teaspoon honey
- 1/2 teaspoon flaked salt
- 1/2 teaspoon freshly ground black pepper

Directions
- Using a spiralizer, cut pear into thin strands.
- Spread 1 tablespoon ricotta on each sourdough slice.
- Cut sliced pear in half and place a half pear on top of riecotta, fanning out the slices.
- Drizzle each with 1/2 teaspoon honey and season with flaked salt and freshly ground black pepper.
- Serve immediately.

Nutritional Information: 1 serving
- 299 calories
- 54g carbs
- 14mg cholesterol
- 5g fat
- 6g protein
- 1031mg sodium

Roasted Beet Strings with Balsamic Goat Cheese Dip

Total time: 20 minutes
Servings: 4

Ingredients
- 2 medium fresh beets, scrubbed, ends trimmed
- 2 tablespoons + 2 teaspoons oil, divided (canola or safflower)
- 1 teaspoon kosher salt
- ¼ teaspoon pepper

Balsamic goat cheese dip:
- 4 ounces goat cheese, crumbled
- ⅓ cup light mayonnaise
- 2 teaspoons balsamic vinegar
- 2 teaspoons honey
- 1 teaspoon fresh thyme leaves
- ¼ teaspoon kosher salt
- ⅛ teaspoon pepper

Directions
- Preheat the oven to 400°F.
- Arrange 2 oven racks to bottom third and upper third of oven.
- Using a spiralizer, cut beet into thin strands.
- Cut spiralized beets into manageable lengths, about 10 - 12 - inches.
- Toss beets in large bowl with 2 tablespoons oil, salt and pepper.
- Rub 1 teaspoon oil on each of two large baking pans and place in hot oven for 3 minutes.
- Remove one preheated pan, spread evenly with half of spiralized beets.
- Repeat with the other pan. Bake approximately 20 - 30 minutes.
- Time will vary depending on size of beets.
- Rotate baking sheets every five minutes.
- Use tongs to toss beet strings as they soften and shrink.
- Remove from oven when a few start to char.
- Allow to cool slightly on baking pan.

Balsamic goat cheese dip:
- Add all dip ingredients to a bowl and mix until combined.

- Mix until dip is whipped and well combined.
- Serve roasted beet strings with dip.

Nutritional Information: 1 serving
- 313 calories
- 13g carbs
- 30mg cholesterol
- 26g fat
- 7g protein
- 1071mg sodium

Shoestring Potatoes with Dipping Sauces

Total time: 30 minutes
Servings: 8

Ingredients
- 2 russet potatoes, ends trimmed
- 2 teaspoons vegetable oil
- 1/2 teaspoon coarse salt

Sriracha Mayo:
- ¼ cup mayonnaise
- 1 teaspoon sriracha

Parsley Pepper Mayo
- ¼ cup mayonnaise
- 1 teaspoon chopped fresh parsley
- 1/2 teaspoon freshly ground black pepper

Directions
- Preheat the oven to 400°F.
- Using a spiralizer, cut potato into thin strands.
- Remove the peel from the bowl.
- Add vegetable oil; toss to coat.
- Spread potatoes in single layer on large baking sheet.
- Bake 18 minutes or until potatoes are golden, stirring once while baking.
- Sprinkle salt over shoestring potatoes; serve immediately with desired dipping sauce.

For the mayos:
- Combine ¼ cup mayonnaise and sriracha in small bowl.
- In a separate small bowl, combine ¼ cup mayonnaise, parsley and black pepper. Refrigerate until ready to use.

Twisted Asparagus Wraps

Total time: 30 minutes
Servings: 20

- **Ingredients**
- nonstick cooking spray
- 10 paper - thin slices prosciutto, cut in half
- 20 medium width asparagus spears, bottom ends trimmed
- 1 medium russet potato, ends trimmed
- 2 tablespoons olive oil
- 3 tablespoons grated parmesan cheese
- ¼ teaspoon pepper

Directions
- Preheat the oven to 425°F.
- Line 2 large baking sheets with parchment paper or spray with nonstick cooking spray.
- Wrap 1/2 slice prosciutto around each asparagus spear starting at corner.
- Set aside.
- Using a spiralizer, cut sweet potato into thin strands.
- Wrap each asparagus spear with a 1/2 - inch spaced potato spiral, trimming potato as needed.
- Arrange on prepared baking sheets.
- Brush lightly with olive oil and sprinkle with Parmesan cheese and pepper.
- Roast for 10 minutes, rotate pans, roast for another 7 -10 minutes (total of 17- 20 minutes) or until the potato is cooked and beginning to brown.
- Serve immediately.

Nutritional Information: 1 serving
- 34 calories
- 3g carbs
- 3mg cholesterol
- 2g fat
- 2g protein
- 67mg sodium

Whole Wheat, Whipped Gorgonzola, Carrots and Roasted Beet

Total time: 50 minutes
Servings: makes 25 crostini

Ingredients
- 1 whole wheat baguette, cut diagonally in 1/2 - inch slices
- 6 tablespoons olive oil, divided
- 3/4 teaspoon kosher salt, divided
- 1/2 teaspoon pepper, divided
- 1 large beet, scrubbed and ends trimmed
- 2 large carrots (1 1/2 - 2"diameter), peeled and ends trimmed

Whipped Gorgonzola:
- 1 teaspoon minced fresh rosemary
- 8 ounces reduced fat cream cheese
- 1/2 cup crumbled Gorgonzola
- zest of half a lemon
- 1 tablespoon lemon juice

Garnish:
- ¼ cup toasted chopped walnuts
- 2 tablespoons thinly sliced chives
- Olive oil to taste

Directions
- Preheat the oven to 350°F.
- Arrange baguette slices on half - sheet baking pan.
- Lightly brush both sides of baguette slices with 2 tablespoons olive oil and sprinkle with ¼ teaspoon salt and ¼ teaspoon pepper.
- Toast in oven 6 minutes, turn toasts over and bake another 6 minutes or until lightly browned.
- Remove from oven and allow to cool.
- Increase oven temperature to 400°F.
- Line a half – sheet baking pan with parchment or spray with nonstick cooking spray.
- Using a spiralizer, cut beet into thin strands.
- Repeat with carrots, using a separate bowl to hold spiralized carrots.

- Toss spiralized carrots with 1 tablespoon olive oil, ¼ teaspoon salt, ⅛ teaspoon pepper and 1/2 teaspoon rosemary.
- Arrange carrots on one side of prepared pan.
- Repeat process with spiralized beets.
- Arrange beets on the other side of the pan to prevent bleeding of beets onto carrots.
- Roast for 12 -15 minutes or until tender and starting to brown.

Whipped Gorgonzola:
- Add remaining olive oil, cream cheese, Gorgonzola, lemon zest and lemon juice in bowl, mix on speed 2 until combined, then speed 8 until whipped.
- Can be made a day ahead.
- Store in refrigerator.
- Assemble crostini by spreading each toast with 2 teaspoons whipped Gorgonzola, top with roasted beets and carrots.
- Sprinkle with walnuts and chives.
- Drizzle with olive oil, to taste.

Nutritional Information: 1 serving
- 85 calories
- 5g carbs
- 7mg cholesterol
- 6g fat
- 2g protein
- 183mg sodium

Sides Recipes

Black Radish Noodles with Anchovy Butter

Total time: 20 minutes
Servings: 4

Ingredients
- 4 black radishes, ends trimmed
- 2 tablespoons olive oil, divided
- 2 ounce can anchovy filets, drained
- 2 cloves garlic
- 1 tablespoon fresh lemon juice
- 2 teaspoons butter
- 1 teaspoon grated lemon peel

Directions
- Cut the radish into strips using a spiralizer
- Combine 1 tablespoon olive oil, anchovies, garlic, lemon juice, butter and lemon peel in a food processor; pulse until finely chopped.
- Heat remaining 1 tablespoon olive oil in large skillet.
- Add radishes; sauté 5 minutes.
- Add anchovy mixture; cook 1- 2 minutes or until radishes are evenly coated with anchovy mixture.
- Divide radish noodles evenly onto 4 plates. Serve immediately.

Nutritional Information: 1 serving
- 160 calories
- 15g carbs
- 15mg cholesterol
- 10g fat
- 5g protein
- 105mg sodium

Domino Potatoes with Sour Cream and Chives

Total time: 1 hour
Servings: 4

Ingredients
- 4 large Idaho potatoes, peeled
- 4 ounces clarified butter
- sea salt
- 4 bay leaves
- 1/2 cup sour cream
- 1 tablespoon chopped chives

Directions
- Preheat the oven to 425°F.
- Line a baking pan with parchment paper.
- Cut potatoes into strips using the spiralizer.
- Place the sliced potatoes on the prepared baking pan.
- Brush with clarified butter, season with salt and insert 1 bay leaf in between the center slices of each potato.
- Bake until potatoes pierce easily with a fork, and edges are golden brown, about 30 - 35 minutes.
- Remove from oven.
- Serve immediately with sour cream and chives.

Nutritional Information: 1 serving
- 498 calories
- 69g carbs
- 60mg cholesterol
- 23g fat
- 9g protein
- 187mg sodium

Hasselbacks with Cheddar Cheese

Total time: 1 hour 15 minutes
Servings: 6

Ingredients
- nonstick cooking spray
- 6 medium yellow potatoes, ends trimmed
- 6 tablespoons butter
- 2 cloves garlic, minced
- 1 teaspoon chopped fresh herbs such as rosemary, thyme or parsley
- 1 teaspoon salt
- ¼ teaspoon freshly ground black pepper
- 1 cup shredded cheddar cheese
- 4 slices bacon, crisp cooked and crumbled

Directions
- Preheat the oven to 400°F.
- Prepare a large rimmed baking sheet with nonstick cooking spray.
- Bring large saucepan of salted water to a boil.
- Cut potato into strips using spiralizer
- Carefully add sliced potatoes to boiling water with a slotted spoon; cook 4 minutes.
- Remove with slotted spoon and drain on paper towels.
- Let sit for 10 minutes.
- Arrange potatoes on prepared baking sheet, separating potato slices slightly.
- In small saucepan over low heat, melt butter.
- Add garlic, herbs, salt and pepper to butter and mix together.
- Remove from heat and brush butter mixture over each potato.
- Bake 30 - 35 minutes or until potatoes are fork-tender and edges are crisp, basting with butter mixture every 10 minutes.
- Remove potatoes from oven and sprinkle with cheese and bacon; bake an additional 5 minutes or until cheese is melted.

Nutritional Information: 1 serving

- 350 calories
- 31g carbs
- 55mg cholesterol
- 19g fat
- 11g protein
- 610mg sodium

Pickled Red Onions and Radishes Sweet and Spicy

Total time: 25 minutes
Servings: 6

Ingredients
- 1 medium red onion, peeled, ends trimmed
- 6 radishes, ends trimmed
- 1 cup apple cider vinegar
- 2 tablespoons sugar
- 1 teaspoon kosher salt
- 2 cloves garlic, sliced
- 1/2 teaspoon black peppercorns
- ¼ teaspoon red pepper flakes
- 1 jalapeño pepper, cored, seeded and sliced

Directions
- Cut onions and radishes into strips using spiralizer
- Coarsely chop the onion and radish strips; return to bowl.
- Combine vinegar, sugar and salt in small saucepan.
- Cook over medium - high heat until sugar and salt are dissolved, stirring frequently.
- Add jalapeño, garlic, peppercorns and red pepper flakes.
- Pour over vegetables; let stand at room temperature 1 hour, stirring occasionally.
- Store in air tight jar in refrigerator for 2 weeks.
NOTE: Serve with tacos, burgers and sandwiches.

Sweet Potatoes with Garlic Mayo

Total time: 35 minutes
Servings: 4

Ingredients
- 4 large sweet potatoes, cut into 4 - inch sections, ends trimmed
- 4 tablespoons butter
- 1/2 teaspoon cayenne
- 1 teaspoon ground cumin
- 1/2 teaspoon sea salt

Garlic Mayo:
- 1/2 cup prepared mayonnaise
- 2 cloves roasted garlic, smashed
- 1 teaspoon parsley, chopped
- freshly ground black pepper

Directions
- Preheat oven to 425°F
- Butter 8 x 8 - inch casserole dish.
- Set aside.
- Cut sweet potato into strips using a spiralizer
- Place the sliced sweet potatoes into casserole dish.
- Melt butter in small sauce pan.
- Add cayenne and cumin.
- Brush seasoned butter over sweet potatoes and sprinkle with sea salt.
- Place in oven, bake 20 - 30 minutes until crisp.

Garlic Mayo:
- Combine mayonnaise, garlic, parsley and black pepper in small bowl.
- Refrigerate until ready to use.
- Serve sweet potatoes with garlic mayo immediately after baking.

Nutritional Information: 1 serving

- 332 calories
- 34g carbs
- 38mg cholesterol
- 21g fat
- 3g protein
- 653mg sodium

Thai Cucumber Relish

Total time: 10 minutes
Servings: 6

Ingredients
- 1 cup unseasoned rice vinegar
- 3 tablespoons sugar
- 1 serrano pepper, seeded and minced
- 2 tablespoons chopped fresh cilantro
- 2 large english cucumbers, ends trimmed, cut into 4 - inch sections
- 1 small red onion, peeled, ends trimmed

Directions
- Combine vinegar and sugar in small bowl; stir to dissolve sugar.
- Add serrano pepper and cilantro.
- Set aside.
- Cut cucumber into strips using spiralizer
- Pour vinegar mixture over vegetables; stir to coat.
- Let stand at room temperature 1- 2 hours for flavors to blend.
- Store in air tight jar in refrigerator.
- Can be made 2 days ahead.

NOTE: Serve with seared salmon or chicken satay.

Nutritional Information: 1/2 serving
- 20 calories
- 5g carbs
- 0mg cholesterol
- 0g fat
- 0g protein
- 0mg sodium

Bonus Recipes!

Zucchini Noodles and Lemon Ricotta

Prep time: 20 minutes
Servings: 2
Ingredients

- 2-3 large zucchini
- 1 cup cherry or grape tomatoes, sliced in half
- olive oil, for drizzling
- sea salt and freshly ground black pepper
- hemp seeds & microgreens, for garnish (optional)

Lemon-Macadamia Ricotta:

- ½ cup raw macadamia nuts, soaked at least 4 hours
- ¼ cup raw sunflower seeds, soaked at least 4 hours
- ¼ cup hemp seeds
- 2 tablespoons fresh lemon juice + ½ teaspoon zest
- 1 tablespoon white wine vinegar
- 1 small garlic clove
- handful of fresh herbs - basil, mint, oregano or tarragon
- ½ teaspoon sea salt
- ¾ cup water, more as needed

Directions

- Drain and rinse your macadamia nuts and sunflower seeds that have been soaking.
- Add them to a high speed blender with hemp seeds, lemon juice, lemon zest, white wine vinegar, garlic, herbs, salt and pepper, and water.
- Add a little olive oil, if necessary, to get your blade moving.
- Use a spiralizer to cut the zucchini into noodle-sized shapes. (You could also use a regular vegetable peeler - peel thin strips and then slice them vertically.)
- Toss zucchini "noodles," with a few spoonfuls of the ricotta, the tomatoes, a drizzle of olive oil and a few pinches of salt and pepper.
- Serve with extra ricotta on the side.
- Extra ricotta will keep in the fridge for about 1 day.
- If it gets a little watery on day 2, give it a stir until it's cohesive again.

Zoodles Cacio e Pepe

Total time: 20 minutes
Servings: 2

Ingredients
- 3 strips of bacon
- 1 large garlic clove, minced
- 1 pinch of red pepper flakes
- 3 medium zucchinis, spiralized
- freshly cracked black pepper, from a grinder
- 1/4 cup grated pecorino romano cheese
- 1/4 cup grated parmigiano reggiano cheese + more to garnish

Directions
- Place a large skillet over medium heat and coat lightly with cooking spray.
- Add in the bacon and cook for 3-5 minutes and then flip over, cooking for another 2-3 minutes.
- Once done, remove and place on a paper-towel lined plate.
- Remove all of the oil from the bacon except for 2 tablespoons.
- Add in the garlic and red pepper flakes and cook for 30 seconds.
- Then, add in the zucchini noodles and toss to cook, for about 2-3 minutes.
- Season the zucchini with about 5 cracks of the pepper and add in the cheeses.
- Toss to combine thoroughly and then plate into two bowls.
- Top each bowl with a few more cranks of black pepper and crumble over a piece and a half of bacon in each bowl.
- Garnish with additional parmigiano reggiano cheese.

Zucchini Caprese Salad

Total time: 20 minutes
Servings: 2

Ingredients

- 2 medium zucchini, spiralized to look like ribbons, then noodles trimmed to 5 inches or less
- 1 cup cherry or cocktail tomatoes, halved

For the marinade:

- 1 tablespoon lemon juice
- 3 tablespoons balsamic vinegar
- 2 tablespoons olive oil
- 1 medium garlic clove, minced
- kosher salt and freshly ground black pepper
- 12 small mozzarella balls, halved
- ½ cup thinly sliced basil leaves

Directions

- Place the zucchini and tomatoes in a large bowl.
- Make the marinade.
- Pulse the ingredients in a food processor until the garlic is smooth.
- Pour the marinade over the zucchini noodles and tomatoes, and toss to combine.
- Place in the refrigerator to marinate for at least 10 minutes.
- Add the mozzarella and basil to the zucchini noodles, toss to combine, and serve.

Zoodle and Carrot Lo Mein

Prep time: 15 minutes
Servings: 4

Ingredients
- 2 teaspoons toasted sesame oil
- 3 green onions, sliced into thin rounds (white and light green parts), (1/3 cup)
- 1 clove garlic, minced
- 6 tablespoons light teriyaki sauce
- 2 teaspoons cornstarch
- 1 teaspoon fresh grated ginger, or ½ teaspoon dried ginger
- 3 medium carrots (12 ounces), spiralized (2 cups)
- 3 large zucchini (about 2 pounds), spiraled into 6-inch strands (11 cups)
- ¾ cup frozen shelled edamame, cooked according to package directions
- 1 cup roughly chopped rotisserie chicken (about 6 ounces)
- roasted, unsalted peanuts, coarsely chopped, optional

Directions
- Heat the oil in a wok or large nonstick skillet over medium-low heat.
- Add the green onions and garlic and cook, stirring frequently until the onions are softened and the garlic is fragrant, about 3 minutes.
- Meanwhile, in a small bowl, whisk together the teriyaki, cornstarch, and ginger until well combined.
- Add the sauce and the zucchini and carrot noodles to the wok, stirring frequently.
- Increase the heat to medium high and cook, stirring frequently, until the noodles soften, about 7 minutes.
- Stir in the edamame and chicken until heated through, about 1 minute.
- Serve with chopped peanuts as desired.

Nutritional Information: 1 serving

- 200 calories
- 6g fat
- 1g saturated fat
- 21g carbohydrates
- 680mg sodium
- 5g fiber
- 20g protein

Ginger Miso Carrots with Watercress and Baked Tofu

Total time: 45 minutes
Servings: 2

Ingredients
For the tofu:
- 6.5 oz extra-firm tofu
- ¼ cup low-sodium soy sauce
- 1 teaspoon sesame oil
- For the salad:
- 2 large carrots
- 3 cups watercress
- ½ teaspoon black sesame seeds + ½ teaspoon white sesame seeds, mixed

For the dressing:
- 2 tablespoons extra virgin olive oil (or avocado oil, if you have it)
- 2 tablespoons rice vinegar
- 1 teaspoon white miso
- ½ tablespoon sesame oil
- ½ inch piece of ginger, grated
- 1 tablespoon of water
- salt and pepper, to taste

Directions
- Preheat the oven to 350 degrees.
- Line a baking sheet with parchment paper and set aside.
- Press excess moisture out of the tofu by squeezing between two layers of paper towels (or other preferred method.)
- Repeat until moisture is absorbed.
- Dice the tofu into cubes and place in a medium mixing bowl along with the other ingredients for the tofu.
- Let marinate for 10 minutes and then arrange on the prepared baking tray.
- While the tofu marinates, combine all the ingredients for the dressing and whisk together until combined.
- Bake the tofu for 30 minutes or until browned and stiffened, flipping the tofu pieces over halfway through.
- While tofu bakes, peel and spiralize the carrots.

- Then, place the carrot noodles into a large mixing bowl and set aside.
- 10 minutes before the tofu is done cooking, drizzle the dressing over the carrot noodles and toss to combine.
- Place in the refrigerator until the tofu is done.
- Once the tofu is done, add the watercress to the bowl with the carrots.
- Toss to combine and then plate the salad, top with tofu and garnish with sesame seed mix.

Nutritional Information: 1 serving
- 308 calories
- 25g total fat
- 0mg cholesterol
- 680mg sodium
- 371mg potassium
- 3g sugars
- 12g protein

Healthy Stir Fried Singapore Noodles

Total time: 30 minutes
Servings: 4

Ingredients
For the Stir Fry
- 4 ounces thin rice noodles
- 1 tablespoon oil
- 2 bell peppers, spiralized
- 2 shallots, thinly sliced
- 1 cup bean sprouts
- 1 teaspoon curry powder
- 1 cup sliced shiitake mushrooms
- 1 cup frozen peas
- sliced scallions for topping

For the Sauce:
- 1 cup low sodium chicken broth (vegetable broth for vegan/vegetarian)
- ¼ cup low sodium soy sauce
- 3 tablespoons mirin
- 2 teaspoons minced garlic
- 1 teaspoon minced ginger (I used a ginger paste)
- ½ teaspoon sambal oelek (adds spiciness - more to taste)

Directions
- Soak the rice noodles in a large bowl of cold water.
- Wash and cut all the vegetables.
- Mix the ingredients for the sauce in a small bowl and set aside.
- Heat the oil in a large skillet over high heat.
- Add the peppers, shallots, and bean sprouts, and curry powder; stir fry for 3-5 minutes.
- Add the mushrooms and the peas; stir fry for 2 minutes.
- The vegetables should be bright and tender-crisp.
- Drain the water from the rice noodles and add the noodles to the pan with the vegetables.
- Add a little splash of sauce - about 2-3 tablespoons - and stir fry, moving the noodles around in the pan continuously so they don't stick together in one big lump - they should move freely and easily.

- After a few minutes of stir frying, remove the pan from heat.
- Once off the heat, add the sauce in small increments, tossing/stirring the noodles in between each addition, until the desired "sauciness" level is reached.
- The goal is for the sauce to thicken slightly when combined with the other ingredients and cling to the noodles instead of soaking into the noodles.
- Top with scallions and more sauce.

Nutritional Information: 1 serving
- 248 calories
- 4.1g total fats
- 0mg cholesterol
- 772mg sodium
- 8.2g proteins

Creamy Spinach Sweet Potato Noodles with Cashew Sauce

Total time: 20 minutes

Servings: 4 - 6
Ingredients
- 1 cup cashews
- ¾ cup water (more for soaking)
- ½ teaspoon salt
- 1 clove garlic
- 1 tablespoon oil
- 4 large sweet potatoes, spiralized
- 2 cups baby spinach
- a handful of fresh basil leaves, chives, or other herbs
- salt and pepper to taste
- olive oil for drizzling

Directions
- Cover the cashews with water in a bowl and soak for 2 hours or so.
- Drain and rinse thoroughly.
- Place in a food processor or blender (I got better texture with the blender) and add the ¾ cup water, salt, and garlic.
- Puree until very smooth.
- Heat the oil in a large skillet over high heat.
- Add the sweet potatoes; toss in the pan for 6-7 minutes with tongs until tender-crisp.
- Remove from heat and toss in the spinach - it should wilt pretty quickly.
- Add half of the herbs and half of the sauce to the pan and toss to combine.
- Add water if the mixture is too sticky.
- Season generously with salt and pepper, drizzle with olive oil, and top with the remaining fresh herbs.

Nutritional Information: 1 serving

- 369 calories
- 18.5g total fats
- 0g cholesterol
- 9.4 g protein
- 401.6mg sodium

Peas and Pesto Potato Noodles

Total time: 40 minutes
Servings: 4

- **Ingredients**
- 1 tablespoon extra virgin olive oil
- 1.5 pounds yukon gold potatoes, spiralized
- salt and pepper, to taste
- 1 cup frozen garden peas
- For the pesto:
- 2 tablespoons pine nuts
- 2 packed cups of basil
- 2 tablespoons parmesan cheese
- 3 tablespoons extra virgin olive oil
- 1 large garlic clove
- salt and pepper, to taste

Directions
- Place a large skillet over medium-high heat and add in the olive oil.
- Once oil heats, add in the potato noodles and season with salt and pepper.
- Toss and then cover and cook, uncovering occasionally to toss, for 7-10 minutes or until potato noodles are cooked through.
- Place in a large mixing bowl.
- While the potatoes cook, in a food processor, place all of the ingredients for the pesto and pulse until creamy.
- Taste and adjust to your preferences, if necessary.
- Set aside.
- Also, cook your peas according to package directions.
- Once potato noodles, peas and pesto are done, combine in a bowl and toss thoroughly to combine.
- Serve immediately or place in refrigerator and serve later, chilled.

Nutritional Information: 1 serving
- 183 calories
- 7g total fat
- 3mg cholesterol
- 96mg sodium
- 3g dietary fiber
- 4g sugars
- 6g protein

Spiralized Sweet Potato Enchilada Casserole

Total time: 1 hour 15 minutes
Servings: 6

Ingredients
- 2 cups cooked chicken, shredded
- 2 cups red enchilada sauce (store-bought or homemade)
- 1 can (15 oz) black beans with no salt added, drained and rinsed
- 1 can (15 oz) corn, drained
- salt and pepper, to taste
- 2 medium sweet potatoes, spiralized
- 6 oz Colby jack cheese or cheese blend, shredded
- 1 green onion, chopped
- ½ avocado, chopped
- parsley, for garnish
- sour cream, for serving

Directions
- Preheat the oven to 400 degrees Fahrenheit.
- Add the shredded chicken, enchilada sauce, black beans, and corn to a large mixing bowl.
- Gently stir to combine.
- Season with salt and pepper, to taste.
- Set aside.
- Lightly spray a 9 x 13 inch casserole dish with cooking spray.
- Add the spiralized sweet potatoes.
- Then, pour the shredded chicken mixture over the sweet potatoes and top with shredded cheese.
- Cover tightly with aluminum foil.
- Bake in the preheated oven for 50 minutes to 1 hour, until the cheese is bubbly and the sweet potatoes are cooked through.
- Remove the aluminum foil for the last 10 minutes of cooking.
- Allow the casserole to rest a few minutes before serving.
- Top with green onions, avocado, parsley, and sour cream.

Parmesan Squash Rice Risotto with Asparagus and Green Peas

Total time: 20 minutes
Servings: 6

Ingredients
- 1 butternut squash, peeled, Blade C
- 1 tablespoon olive oil
- cooking spray
- 6-8 stalks of asparagus, cut into thirds salt and pepper
- 1/4 cup diced red onion (or white)
- 1 cup + 2 tablespoons vegetable broth
- 1/2 cup grated parmesan cheese
- 1/4 cup cooked green peas

Directions
- Place your butternut squash noodles (in batches) into a spiralizer and slice them into several strips.
- Once done, set aside the butternut squash noodle rice into a bowl.
- Place a large skillet over medium heat and coat with cooking spray.
- Add in the asparagus, lightly spray with cooking spray and season with salt and pepper.
- Cook, stirring frequently, until asparagus turns bright green and is soft when forked.
- Set aside.
- While the asparagus is cooking, place another large skillet over medium-low heat and add in the olive oil.
- Once the oil heats, add in the garlic, cook for 30 seconds and then add in the onion.
- Cook until the onion starts to soften.
- Add in 2 tablespoons of the vegetable broth and let reduce.
- Then, add in the squash rice, season with salt and pepper and stir.
- Add in 1/2 cup of vegetable broth and let reduce.
- Once reduced, add in another 1/2 cup of vegetable broth and let reduce.
- At this point, taste test the risotto.

- If the squash rice needs to cook more, add another 1/2 cup of broth.
- If it's cooked enough, add in the parmesan cheese, stir to combine and let cook for 30 seconds or until cheese melts fully into the squash rice.
- Add the asparagus and peas to the skillet with the risotto and stir to combine.
- Pour into bowls and enjoy!

Cold Spaghetti Squash Salad

Total time: 3 hours
Servings: 3

Ingredients
- 1 spaghetti squash, halved and seeded
- 8 ounces cherry tomatoes, halved
- 6 ounces pitted kalamata olives, halved
- 2 english cucumbers - spiralized
- 1 small red onion, sliced thin
- 1 clove garlic, minced
- 1/4 cup lemon juice
- 1 tablespoon lemon zest
- 1/4 cup olive oil, or more if needed
- 1 tablespoon garlic salt
- ground black pepper to taste

Directions
- Preheat an oven to 350 degrees F (175 degrees C).
- Place the squash halves into a large baking dish with the cut-sides facing down.
- Bake in the preheated oven until you can easily cut into the skin side with a knife, about 30 minutes; remove from oven and set aside to cool.
- Toss the cooled spaghetti squash, the tomatoes, olives, cucumbers, red onion, and garlic together in a large bowl until evenly mixed.
- Stir the lemon juice and lemon zest together in a small bowl; slowly pour the olive oil into the lemon juice mixture while whisking vigorously.
- Season with garlic salt and pepper; drizzle over the spaghetti squash mixture and toss to coat.
- Refrigerate at least 2 hours before serving.

Summer Squash Shakshuka with Baked Eggs

Total time: 20 minutes
Servings: 4

Ingredients
- 2 pounds summer squash (zucchini, yellow squash, pattypan, etc.)
- 1 tablespoon kosher salt, plus more for sprinkling
- 2 tablespoons + 2 teaspoons olive oil, divided
- 2 medium shallots, sliced
- 2 cloves garlic, minced
- 1/4 teaspoon smoked paprika, plus more for sprinkling
- 1/2 pound tomatoes, chopped
- 4 ounces soft goat cheese
- 1/4 cup loosely packed chiffonade of basil, plus more for garnish
- 4 large eggs
- freshly ground black pepper

Directions
- Slice the squash into strips using a spiralizer.
- Combine with 1 tablespoon salt in a colander and let drain in the sink for 30 minutes.
- Preheat the oven to 375°F. In an oven-safe skillet, warm 2 tablespoons olive oil over medium heat.
- Add the shallots, garlic, and paprika and cook, stirring, until just tender and fragrant.
- Squeeze as much liquid as possible from the squash with your hands and add it to the skillet along with the tomatoes.
- Cook, stirring occasionally, until the mixture is tender and no longer releasing liquid, about 10 minutes.
- Remove the skillet from heat and stir in goat cheese and basil.
- Smooth the mixture evenly in the skillet and make four wells using the back of a spoon.
- Pour 1/2 teaspoon olive oil in each well.
- One at a time, crack an egg into a small bowl and pour into one of the wells.
- Sprinkle salt, pepper, and paprika over each egg.

- Bake until egg whites are set and yolks are still soft, about 10 minutes.
- Garnish with basil and serve with crusty bread.

Nutritional Information: 1 serving
- 297 calories
- 30.3g fat
- 15.9g carbs
- 9.1g sugars
- 15.7g proteins
- 199mg cholesterol

Chicken Piccata with Butternut Squash Noodles

Total time: 40 minutes
Servings: 4

Ingredients
For the butternut squash:
- 1 medium butternut squash, spiralized
- olive oil, to drizzle
- 1 teaspoon garlic powder
- salt and pepper, to taste

For the chicken:
- 1 egg, beaten
- 2 skinless and boneless chicken breast, butterflied and then cut in half
- salt and pepper, to taste
- ⅓ cup freshly squeezed lemon juice
- ½ cup chicken stock, low sodium
- ¼ cup capers, rinsed
- ¼ cup freshly chopped parsley

For the breading:
- ¾ cup almond meal
- ½ teaspoon garlic powder
- salt and pepper, to taste
- ½ teaspoon dried parsley flakes
- ½ teaspoon dried oregano flakes
- ¼ teaspoon onion powder

Directions
- Preheat the oven to 400 degrees.
- Meanwhile, spread the butternut squash noodles out on a baking sheet, drizzle with (optional) olive oil and season with garlic powder, salt and pepper.
- Bake the noodles for 8-10 minutes or until al dente, tossing halfway through.
- While the butternut squash cooks, place the egg into a shallow dish and then combine all of the ingredients for the breading into another shallow dish, making sure to mix thoroughly.

- Dip each chicken portion into the egg and then dip both sides into the breading mixture to coat. Set aside on a clean plate and season with salt and pepper.
- Place a large skillet over medium-high heat and add in the olive oil.
- Once oil heats, add in the chicken and cook for 3 minutes, flip and cook for another 3-5 minutes or until cooked all the way through.
- Remove and transfer to a plate, leaving in all the juices.
- Immediately add in the lemon juice, stock and capers.
- Bring to a boil and scraupe up the brown bits from the pan.
- Add the chicken back to the pan and simmer for 5 minutes.
- Remove the chicken and transfer to a platter.
- Stir in the parsley to the sauce and remove the pan from heat.
- Divide the finished butternut squash noodles into four plates or bowls and top with chicken.
- Pour over extra sauce from the pan.
- Serve immediately.

Nutritional Information: 1 serving
- 312 calories
- 72mg cholesterol
- 18g total fat
- 4g sugars
- 20g protein

Made in the USA
San Bernardino, CA
17 January 2017